Michel Zink

Université de Paris IV — Sorbonne

Medieval French Literature: An Introduction

MEDIEVAL & RENAISSANCE TEXTS & STUDIES

VOLUME 110

_____

PEGASUS PAPERBOOKS

NUMBER 19

_____

Michel Zink

Université de Paris IV — Sorbonne

Medieval French Literature:
An Introducton

Translated by

Jeff Rider

MEDIEVAL & RENAISSANCE TEXTS & STUDIES
Binghamton, New York
1995

Library of Congress Cataloging-in-Publication Data

Zink, Michel.
    [Littérature française. English]
    Medieval French literature : an introduction / Michel Zink ; translated
by Jeff Rider.
       p. cm. — (Medieval & Renaissance texts & studies ; vol. 110)
(Pegasus paperbooks)
    Includes bibliographical references and index.
    ISBN 0–86698–163–2 (MRTS). — ISBN 0–86698–161–6 (Pegasus)
    1. French literature—To 1500—History and criticism. I. Title.
II. Series.
PQ151.Z5313 1994
840.9'001—dc20   93–47138
                                                           CIP

This book is made to last.
It is set in Plantin
and printed on acid-free paper
to library specifications

Printed in the United States of America

Contents

Contents

The Question of Celtic Sources: The Breton Lay
Tristan and Isolde
The "Breton" Romance and the Heritage of Chrétien
The Many Paths of Adventure

Part Three: The Establishment of a Literature 67

Chapter 6. The Birth of Prose: Romance and Chronicle 69
The First Prose Romances
Chronicles: From Latin to French, from Verse to Prose
Chapter 7. Drama and Laughter 77
The Dramatic Expression of Literature
Theater
The *Dit*: A Birth of Poetry
The *Fabliaux*
The *Roman de Renart*
Chapter 8. Allegory 90
Medieval Allegory: Rhetoric and Exegesis
Allegory and Personification before the *Roman de la Rose*
The *Roman de la Rose*
The Influence of the *Roman de la Rose*

Part Four: The End of the Middle Ages 101

Chapter 9. Poetry in the Fourteenth and Fifteenth 103
Centuries
The New Rules of the Lyric Game
Guillaume de Machaut and His Heirs
Charles d'Orléans
Villon
The *Grands Rhétoriqueurs*
Chapter 10. The Forms of Reflection: Testimony, 116
Judgement, Knowledge
War and History
Political Thought
Didacticism
From Clerk to Humanist
Chapter 11. The Forms of Representation 126
The Representation of a World

Contents

Translator's Note

This book is substantially the same as that which appeared in 1990 from the Presses Universitaires de Nancy under the title *Littérature Française—Le Moyen Age*. The Conclusion has been taken from a longer version of the French book which appeared in 1992 from the Presses Universitaires de France under the title *Littérature française du Moyen Age*. I have also added some footnotes for the reader's convenience and expanded both the original Bibliography and the Chronology.

I would like to thank Michel Zink for the compliment he has paid me by permitting me to translate his work, for his help in the preparation of the translation, and for forgiving me the betrayals and deformations of both his thought and his style into which I have inevitably been forced.

I would also like to thank Professor Peggy McCracken of the University of Illinois-Chicago, Professors Karen Bock and Gary Shaw of Wesleyan University, and Gina Wilcox for their willingness to read over the translation and their helpful suggestions. I am likewise indebted to Professor Mario Di Cesare, director of Medieval & Renaissance Texts & Studies, and to MRTS's readers for their suggestions and comments.

Finally, I wish to acknowledge the general help and encouragement of my colleagues in the Medieval Studies Program at Wesleyan University and thank them for creating such a productive environment in which to work.

Jeff Rider

Foreword

David Staines

Michel Zink is professor of medieval French literature at the University of Paris-Sorbonne and one of the foremost scholars in the field. Currently he is director of two literary series, "Lettres Gothiques" published by Livre de Poche and the medieval collection published by the Société d'Editions d'Enseignement Supérieur Réunis [SEDES], and co-director of a third, "Perspectives littéraires" published by the Presses Universitaires de France. Among the many books of which he is author or editor are *La Pastourelle: Poésie et folklore au moyen âge* (1972), *La Prédication en langue romane avant 1300* (1976), *Les Chansons de toile* (1978), *Roman rose et rose rouge: Le Roman de la Rose ou de Guillaume de Dole de Jean Renart* (1979), *Le Roman d'Apollonius de Tyr* (1982), *La Subjectivité littéraire: autour du siècle de saint Louis* (1985), the complete works of Rutebeuf (1989–90), and *Dictionnaire des lettres françaises: Le moyen âge* (1992).

By means of—not in spite of—his immense knowledge of medieval French literature, Zink makes *Medieval French Literature: An Introduction* a personal (though not autobiographical) odyssey through four centuries of literary accomplishments. Adopting a socio-historical approach, he proves himself a supreme "generalist," a term too often in disrepute now, whose inquiries take him through a landscape of his own knowledge towards an understanding of the development of a literary culture. And this quest, so distinctly and appropriately medieval, is undertaken with an honesty and a humility too rare in contemporary criticism.

As he starts out, Zink cautions us:

A beginning: this is the source of the fascination medieval literature exercises on the mind—a fascination founded on the impression, or the illusion, that the past explains the present, that the truth of what we are is to be found further back in time, deeper in the roots. A beginning that is not really a beginning: this is the source of the complexity and the originality of medieval literature.

While he invites us to join his quest, he never allows us to lose sight of the complexity and the originality of his subject. As he moves from period to period, from genre to genre, he examines his material in order to open it up, never to categorize simplistically or to simplify. For me, the achievement of *Medieval French Literature* is that its exploration illuminates its subject, raises new critical questions, and leaves the reader to continue the exploration.

Invoking though not necessarily subscribing to evolutionary theory, Zink establishes a fourfold chronological division of French literature in the Middle Ages: "Les conditions d'une genèse" ("The Conditions of a Genesis"); "L'épanouissement" ("The Blossoming"); "La constitution d'une littérature" ("The Establishment of a Literature"); and "La fin du moyen âge" ("The End of the Middle Ages"). These divisions are, as he proves, "not arbitrary and can be made to coincide, without artifice, with the stages of a reasonable and coherent account of the development of this literature."

And what a canvas presents itself! Zink begins with the emergence of the French language, noting that there was no guarantee that the language "would become an independent language of culture, and, in particular, of written culture." Then, with his characteristic reminder that critical generalizations are too often simplistic or faulty, he reminds us:

> The somewhat tortuous phrase I have just used—"an independent language of culture, and, in particular, of written culture"—betrays a hesitation and a difficulty. In what sense was writing a criterion of culture in medieval civilization? Did the two oppositions "Latin vs. French" and "writing vs. speaking" correspond exactly?

Zink's journey is our journey, his quest our quest. Will the French language turn out to be the hero of his story? The process of discovery that becomes, for Zink, the history of medieval French literature.

The critical pauses, the hesitations, the qualifications—these are the signs of an informed scholar knowing too well that simple statements, uninformed generalizations, and random observations are inappropriate to a journey of discovery. No sooner does Zink embark on a discussion of early oral culture than he stands back: "Does this mean that we are really dealing with an oral culture where writing was secondary? Nothing could be less true. Admission to the world of writing was cloaked in considerable social and religious status." And then he examines the *seeming* opposition between writing and speaking as well as the *seeming* opposition between learned culture and popular culture.

The opening chapter ends:

> The clerk and the jongleur were thus the two promoters of French literature in its infancy, and their changing relation to this literature throughout the Middle Ages reflects its evolution.
>
> But let us not get ahead of ourselves. Let us return, rather, to the moment when the French language emerged, when it was still up to the clerks to decide whether or not this new language would produce texts.

Thus the story unfolds, the story of a language, a literature, and a scholar's quest.

Medieval French Literature moves from the epic *chansons de geste* and their origins to the romances both verse and later prose. The account includes the advent of courtly lyricism, for which Zink offers a sensible summation of courtly love as the troubadours celebrated it, the development of native drama, and the French employment of allegory. As he enters the last two centuries of the Middle Ages, he cannot find evidence that the political, religious, and social crises brought about a literary decadence. Instead, he examines the courtly poets of this time and their princely services, the growth of historiography (especially in the form of the chronicle) and scientific writing, and then the introduction of Italian humanism into France.

"There was thus no clear rupture, no interruption in theatrical forms at the end of the fifteenth century," Zink observes, "just as there was not in other literary forms." There is no end to the Middle Ages, nor is there an end to their influence on

later centuries in literary as well as other areas. The Middle
Ages are indeed a beginning, an opening which denies an insistence on closure.

Zink arrives at a final caution: "Medieval literature cannot
be approached through the conventional distinctions of other
periods, including our own." But such a caution is no excuse
for intellectual inertia. Zink rightly reminds us of the reason for
his *and* our journey:

> It is not futile to attempt to understand and appreciate this
> literature. First and foremost, because it is pleasurable, but
> also because the discovery of a world which was simulta-
> neously so near and so far from our own invites us to take
> a new look at ourselves.

Medieval French Literature leads to just such a discovery, and
through Jeff Rider's careful and caring translation, many more
readers can embark on Michel Zink's instructive voyage of discovery, for this book widens considerably the readership that
can enjoy the literary riches of the French Middle Ages.

Introduction

French literature first appeared in the Middle Ages. The ages in between, the intermediate ages, the "Middle Ages"— defined thus negatively as the period separating the classical world from the modern world, without a character of their own—were in fact an age of beginnings. Error and truth mingle in the tension between a name that would be offensive were it not so shopworn, and the reality it hides. For it is indeed true that a continuity existed between classical culture and medieval culture, but it is also true that they were separated by a profound rupture. Medieval culture was in many ways, if only by virtue of the appearance of new languages, a true beginning.

A beginning: this is the source of the fascination medieval literature exercises on the mind—a fascination founded on the impression, or the illusion, that the past explains the present, that the truth of what we are is to be found further back in time, deeper in the roots. A beginning that is not really a beginning: this is the source of the complexity and the originality of medieval literature. The Middle Ages are the moment in which we can seize French civilization and literature in their primitive state, and yet medieval French civilization was in no way primitive, even though certain anthropological approaches sometimes permit one to understand it better.

Such is the first ambiguity of this literature. One may see in it a deliberate effort to imitate, develop, and adapt classical models after the ruptures caused by the collapse of the Roman world, the formation of the young romance languages, and the emergence of a feudal society. One may also see it, on the other hand, as essentially a reflection of a new world, of new sensibilities and new forms of expression. Both the one and the other are true, and it is difficult to harmonize these two truths. According to which of these truths one privileges, moreover, the relations between Latin and the vernacular language, between the written and the spoken, between the modern notion of literature and the practices of the time take on different aspects.

All the same—and this is the second difficulty encountered by an introductory study—this literature evolved profoundly over time. How could it have been otherwise? It is not a matter of cutting out and studying a single century in the history of French literature. The Middle Ages stretched out over a thousand years. According to historians, they began with the fall of the western Roman empire in 476 and ended in the second half of the fifteenth century. It may be true that the first monuments of French literature did not appear until the end of the ninth century and that this literature was not really established until the end of the eleventh century, but this still leaves four or five centuries of literary production grouped together under the common name of medieval literature.

The approach that will be followed in this book is based on the large chronological divisions of this long period. It is intended to show that these divisions are not arbitrary and can be made to coincide, without artifice, with the stages of a reasonable and coherent account of the development of this literature. I will first consider, in Part One, the conditions of its genesis in relation to the genesis of the language that was its vehicle, and the first manifestations of this language in the oldest extant texts. Part Two will describe the blossoming of an abundant and original French literature through an investigation of its oldest and most important forms—*chanson de geste* (epic song), lyric poetry, and romances—in the twelfth century. The third part will show how the very success of this literature entailed its mutation and its renewal in certain domains, its sclerosis in others; how this success modified the conditions of intellectual and literary life and the diffusion of the writings; how, more generally, it provoked a profound change in literary consciousness. This evolution occurred more or less during the thirteenth century. The fourth part, finally, will consider the last two centuries of medieval French literature, a period which, without calling into question the literary system established in the second half of the thirteenth century, nonetheless formed in many ways a universe of its own and thus requires separate treatment.

1   *Birth of a Language,
Genesis of a Literature*

Latin and the Vernacular

A single institution survived the Germanic invasions and the
collapse of the Roman Empire and assured the survival of Latin
culture: the Church. At the same time, spoken Latin, introduced into Gaul five centuries earlier as a result of the Roman
conquest, and already having undergone significant changes,
began to change more quickly and more drastically. Several
centuries later, French literature was born of the coming together—sometimes in an alliance, sometimes in a confrontation—of
the young language born from the ruins of Latin and the already ancient Church, curator of Latin letters.

In "going over to the barbarians," converting the Germanic
conquerors, the Church saved itself and saved Latin culture. Its
schools were the only schools. It supplied the courts of the
Gothic sovereigns, fascinated by the Roman chancellory, with
literate officials. Its bishops, like Sidonius Apollinaris in the fifth
century and Venantius Fortunatus in the sixth, still cultivated
the art of poetry, exchanged stiffly elegant letters, and composed panegyrics and epithalamia in nearly correct hexameters
for princes who barely understood them. Without the manuscripts copied and preserved in its monasteries, Latin literature
would be almost entirely lost to us. Under the influence of
monasticism in the sixth and seventh centuries, it is true, the
Church tended to turn in upon itself, to think of itself as an
ideal and autonomous society, to view the lay world as a sort of
necessary evil, and to manifest an ever greater severity towards
worldly literature. Saint Augustine did permit the study of the
liberal arts and pagan authors as preparation for the reading of
sacred texts, but this concession was granted less and less often
as time went on, and it was denied entirely, for example, by the
seventh-century Anglo-Saxon monk the Venerable Bede. Had it

not met with strong resistance, such severity might well have threatened the survival of the classical heritage, preserved until that time alongside of the scriptural and patristic heritage. However, this severity might also be credited with encouraging the extraordinary blossoming of Gregorian chant, a liturgical poetry altogether novel in its form, its expression, and its melodies. As we will see, its poetry and melodies preceded and announced a secular lyricism in the vernacular language. In the second half of the eighth century, the Carolingian renaissance restored classical authors to a place of honor in its efforts to give a better education to the clergy and, therefore, to imperial officials.

But a phenomenon of capital importance occurred at about the same time, one that would slowly but irrevocably define the limits and modify the range of every effort, however fertile, to preserve, restore, and prolong Latinate culture. The spoken language had evolved to the point where the *illiterati*, those who had not been to school, no longer understood Latin. There were no longer two different Latins, literary and spoken, but two different languages. It is hard to know exactly when textual expressions like *lingua rustica* (the rustic language), and so on started to refer to this new language rather than to spoken Latin, but it was certainly the case already in 813, when a canon of the Council of Tours encouraged priests to preach "in linguam rusticam gallicam aut theotiscam" ("in the common 'Gallic' or the common 'Teutonic' language"), or, in other words, in French or in German. At Strasbourg thirty years later, in 842, two of the sons of Louis the Pious, Charles the Bald and Louis the German, and their partisans swore oaths in the Germanic and the Romance languages on the occasion of one of their inconsequential reconciliations, and these oaths were recorded by the historian Nithard in his *Historiarum libri IV* (*Histories*) or *De dissensionibus filiorum Ludovici pii* (*History of the Conflicts of the Sons of Louis the Pious*). Thus was preserved for us the first text in a language that was no longer Latin and would become French.

This evolution was accompanied by fragmentation. Learned from the mouths of legionaries who certainly did not speak like Cicero and who came from every corner of the empire, deformed by native throats, and enriched by Germanic contributions and indigenous residues, spoken Latin did not undergo a uniform transformation. The diversity of phonetic habits, the proportion of the Germanic element of the population, the level to which Latin culture had penetrated and the length of time it had been in place, the relative importance of these different factors, all these varied from region to region. This is why in Romania, in the lands where Roman colonization had been so strong that the new languages were direct descendants of Latin, these languages—the Romance languages—were different from one another. In the territory that is now France, two languages appeared, which since the time of Dante have been referred to by the way to say "yes" in each: the language of *oïl* in the north and the language of *oc* in the south. But these languages themselves were so divided into numerous dialects that contemporaries seem for a long time to have had the impression that there was only one French language and that all the variations were dialectal. A unifying force, literature opposed this centrifugal motion by giving one dialect ascendancy—sometimes only momentary—over the others or, more often, by making a deliberate effort to efface or combine dialectal traces in an attempt to be understood by everyone.

But let us return to the moment when the French language emerged face to face with Latin. It did not become a language of culture simply because it existed; nothing at that time guaranteed that it would ever become one. Or, more precisely, nothing guaranteed that it would become a written language. The Church had a monopoly on intellectual tools and learning. The clerks were all busy copying, commenting on, and imitating the texts of classical authors, adding to the body of scriptural exegesis, composing liturgical poems, and, eventually, reopening the study of philosophy. Why should they seek to forge a new culture in a language that barely existed? Why should they take the trouble to copy down the rude and immoral songs of bumpkins? We know such songs existed because they were condemned as early as the sixth century in sermons and in the ordinances of ecclesiastical councils. And in the tenth century Bernard d'Angers heard them reverberating in the church of Sainte Foy in Conques and was astonished to learn that they pleased the little saint, as she had made known in a vision to an abbot who had wished to silence them. Why should clerks note

down legends in which pagan beliefs still flowered? And if they
didn't do it, who would? Only in the bosom of the Church
could one learn to read and write. And learning to read and
write meant learning to read and write Latin. Even at the very
end of the thirteenth century, after two centuries of a flourish-
ing literature in French and at a time when many lay people in
fact knew how to read vernacular languages without knowing
any, or hardly any, Latin, the Catalan Ramon Lull, in his
educational treatise entitled *Doctrina pueril* (*On the Education of
Children*), considers it a daring innovation to suggest that children be taught to read and write in their first language. When
the French language first emerged, therefore, nothing guaranteed that it would become an independent language of culture,
and, in particular, of written culture. After all, it might well
have remained indefinitely in a situation similar to that in which
dialectal Arabic finds itself vis-à-vis literary Arabic. But things
turned out otherwise, and this is why the appearance of the first
French texts merits the attention I will devote to it in the next
chapter.

Writing and Speaking
The somewhat tortuous phrase I have just used—"an independent language of culture, and, in particular, of written
culture"—betrays a hesitation and a difficulty. In what sense
was writing a criterion of culture in medieval civilization? Did
the two oppositions "Latin vs. French" and "writing vs. speaking" correspond exactly? It is clear that Latin had a monopoly
on writing when the Romance languages appeared, but
throughout the Middle Ages the relation between writing and
speaking was generally very different than it is today, even
though the practice of writing spread continuously during this
period. Oral performance played the essential role more often
than not, and writing seemed to exist only to compensate for
lapses of memory. This was true even in the legal domain: some
original charters do no more than testify to the existence of a
legal action that was performed orally; others merely allude to
an orally performed action without bothering to transcribe the
details of the agreement. The predominance of oral performance is even clearer in the case of literary works. The medieval
literary work, whatever it was, was always intended for oral

transmission and existed only in performance. Song was the es-
sence of poetry, in both Latin and French. Indeed, until romances appeared, all French literature, without exception, was
composed to be sung. Poetry, like prose, was read aloud and,
undoubtedly, was often recited in a sort of musical monotone.
In all this literature there was a theatrical dimension whose importance we will consider later on. Seen from this point of view,
the text is just a part of a work that writing transmits only in a
mutilated form. One should think here of musical notation, of
the neumatic notation of the high Middle Ages which had
neither staff nor indication of key. It did not help to decipher
the melody, but it did help people who already knew the melody to remember it accurately, and in fact gave them indications
that were sometimes astonishingly precise. It would be rather
artificial to push this comparison between musical notation and
the text too far, but it is nonetheless true that the medieval text
was first and foremost a set of essential notes intended to help
a performer remember a work.

Most medieval culture, therefore, was not written; and this
was almost as true for Latin culture as it was for French. It is
generally true that there were far more copies of the most
widely disseminated Latin works than there were of those in
French, but even Latin books were rare. Books were expensive,
and their circulation was limited. A library with fifty volumes
was a rich one. When universities were founded in the thirteenth century, their methods testified to the continuing prima-
cy of the spoken word and the continuing transmission of the
written word through the medium of the voice even in the
highest intellectual circles: a course consisted of the reading
aloud of a text that the students did not have before them,
accompanied by a commentary. And universities so loathed
writing that examinations remained exclusively oral until the
end of the nineteenth century. Therefore, all that can be said is
that Latin was, for good reason, written before French—both
historically and in the life of the educated individual—and that
writers and scribes were also professional Latinists. But whether
it was a matter of transmitting knowledge or enhancing esthetic
effects, speaking held the predominant place in all medieval
culture, Latin as well as vernacular culture, and not just in the
latter.

Does this mean that we are really dealing with an oral culture where writing was secondary? Nothing could be less true. Admission to the world of writing was cloaked in considerable social and religious status. Written documents were cited as sources and authorities: as we will see, the authors of romances and *chansons de geste* (epic songs) systematically claim, truly or falsely, to have a written source, and preferably a Latin one. The authority par excellence was the Bible, the Book, the Scripture. On Judgement Day, sings the *Dies irae* (*Day of Wrath*), salvation or damnation will depend on the written trace of each person's life: "Liber scriptus referetur / In quo totum continetur" ("the written book will be brought in which everything is contained"). And, according to numerous *exempla*, or edifying anecdotes, penitence so thoroughly erased sins from this great holy book that the devil himself forgot them. In the domain of literature proper, the attention paid to the correct transmission of texts belies any indifference, even relative indifference, to writing. Certain texts do preserve traces of orality, but they are ambiguous and difficult to interpret once they have been fossilized in writing. Speaking was essential, but it was also secondary. Performance was a practical necessity in the actualization of a work—in the realization of its potential effects and, in some cases perhaps, but only in an obscure way, in its composition—and in the immediate transmission of knowledge. But writing preserved words, and this made it authoritative. Again, this was as true in the domain of Latin as it was in the domain of French, once the latter began to be written.

still true

Like the opposition between writing and speaking, the opposition between learned culture and popular culture does not altogether correspond to that between Latin and the vernacular. It is true that some popular beliefs and customs entered the world of writing only when clerks mentioned them with distrust or disgust, or at best without understanding them, or when a manual for confessors instructed priests to ask about them in order to condemn them. But this was because the clerks themselves wished to emphasize the differences between their world and that of the *rustici*. In reality, the two types of sensibilities, beliefs, and ways of thinking differed little. The line dividing the two worlds or, more generally, the line dividing cultivated people from uncultivated ones, did not necessarily correspond to the line dividing those who could read and write from those who could not, or even to the line dividing those who knew Latin from those who did not. The traces of a popular culture are more numerous and more precise in Latin texts than in French ones. Lay princes—who could not themselves read and write, who knew Latin barely or not at all, but who had *chansons de geste*, saints' lives, historical or biblical compilations, and romances sung or read to them—were more "cultivated" than the clerical jobber who copied the texts out for them, the merchant who was able to keep his account books and knew his letters and numbers but nothing more, or even the obscure monk, despite his veneer of Latin, who remained locked away in his monastery. These princes were also probably further removed from "popular culture." They were "men of letters" who knew neither how to write nor how to read or who, if they were literate, did not often use their abilities, while many of those who did frequently read and write were actually strangers to the world of letters. Both the former and the latter were, but inversely, both literate and illiterate, depending on whether these terms are understood literally or metaphorically.

There are thus no simple answers to the two questions I asked at the beginning of this section. Was writing a criterion of culture? Yes, undoubtedly, but not rigidly or exclusively, because in the Middle Ages it did not have the autonomy it does today. Its use presumed, rather, a passage through orality. Was writing associated with Latin, speaking with French? No, for the same reason: the medieval world was not a world of pure orality, and writing was never totally self-sufficient there. Yes, however, in one sense, since one could not master Latin without mastering writing, and for a long time it was almost impossible to master writing without mastering Latin. For French, the attainment of written representation was an innovation and a conquest marking, necessarily, the moment French literature first appears to us, although it may of course have had a previous, purely oral, existence.

Clerk and Jongleur

To the two oppositions mentioned above—"Latin vs. French" and "writing vs. speaking"—we need to add a third concerning the authors and the actors of literature: the opposition "clerk vs.

jongleur." A clerk was simultaneously a churchman and someone who could read, someone who could understand texts. The
two ideas were indissolubly united in the name. The opposite of
the clerk, therefore, was the illiterate lay person. Intellectual
activity and spiritual effort were united in the clerk. To him
were attached both the authority of the Scripture and the authority emanating from all books. His language was Latin, the
language of the Church. He was the instrument of the ecclesiastical preservation of Latin literature mentioned earlier. Because
he held a monopoly on writing, the fate of the young French
language was in his hands. He would decide whether it became
a language of written culture or not. In the ninth and tenth
centuries, nothing had been decided. As we will see, however,
the clerks "went over" to French just as the Church had "gone
over" to the barbarians. Most medieval French authors and
scribes were clerks. And many of them, a great many of them,
made no effort to draw French literature in the direction of
their professional preoccupations, religious subjects or the world
of the schools.

Beside the clerk stood writing and the Church. Across from
him stood the jongleur, condemned by the Church, the man—
or the woman—of orality and performance. The word *joculator*
is attested from the sixth century on, and its etymological link
with the modern French *jeu* (play, game, sport) is clear evidence
that the jongleur was an itinerant entertainer, undoubtedly the
heir of the ambulant actors of late antiquity, but perhaps also of
the Celtic bards and the Germanic singers of epic poems. The
jongleur's activities were highly diverse: he or she might be an
acrobat, animal trainer, mime, musician, dancer, or singer. Not
all jongleurs dedicated themselves to the recitation or singing of
poems, but those who did played an important role in the diffusion, and perhaps in the elaboration, of certain poetic forms,
like lyric poetry and especially the *chanson de geste*. Thomas
Cabham's thirteenth-century manual for confessors divided jongleurs into three categories, one of which—the singers of *chansons de geste* and saints' lives—escaped the condemnation he
heaped on the other two. Performers, but sometimes also cre-
ators—the line between the two was not as well defined as has
sometimes been suggested—perpetually in search of a generous
patron, the jongleurs provided the necessary oral and vocal real-

ization of the medieval work. This is why their role diminished as written civilization expanded. From the thirteenth century on, they sought full-time employment with a great lord and held in his court the position of a *ministerialis*, or minstrel. But the true court poets were the *grands rhétoriqueurs*, or great rhetoricians, of the fifteenth century, who were scholars—and clerks.

The clerk and the jongleur were thus the two promoters of French literature in its infancy, and their changing relation to this literature throughout the Middle Ages reflects its evolution.

But let us not get ahead of ourselves. Let us return, rather, to the moment when the French language emerged, when it was still up to the clerks to decide whether or not this new language would produce texts.

2   *The First Texts*

The Church had no particular reason for devoting the competence of its clerks to the service of the young French language in and of itself. But it had to do so. The sons of Louis the Pious had been obliged to resort to the common Germanic and Romance languages in 842 for political reasons, in order that each one might understand the terms of the oath sworn by the other. The Church was forced to resort to the vernacular language for pastoral reasons. The canon of the Council of Tours held in 813, cited above, and similar canons from throughout the ninth century set forth these reasons in their utter simplicity: if it had not been willing to preach to the people in their own language, the Church would have had to renounce its pursuit of their often still incomplete conversion. This desire to preach in a simple language accessible to everyone, and the consequent need to renounce the oratorical elegance so important to Latin literature, had been manifested often even before the separation of Latin and French, as for example, in the sermons of Saint Caesarius of Arles at the very beginning of the sixth century.

A single written witness of this effort to preach in French survives from the period before the true flowering of French literature. It is a fragmentary draft, half in ordinary letters, half in Tironian notation, of a sermon on the conversion of the Ninevites by Jonah preached at Saint-Amand-les-Eaux (near Lille) around 950 on the occasion of a three-day fast undertaken in the hope that the town might thus be delivered from the Normans. The text is nothing more than a paraphrase of Saint Jerome's commentary on the *Book of Jonah*, written partly in Latin, partly in French. The author was evidently more familiar with French than with Latin, for the only sentence entirely of his own making (on the ultimate conversion of the Jews, a subject dear to his heart) is also the only sentence entirely in French. He was so dependent on his Latin model, however, that, when he followed it, he could not keep himself from ending in Latin sentences he had begun in French. The text thus shows that habits and cultural models were stronger than simple linguistic competence.

Of course, the humble homilies composed for the people in their own language were not intended to be written down. The sermon on Jonah has come down to us only in the form of a rough copy. In general, sermons in French were not written down and no attention was paid to the esthetic resources or literary potential of these entirely utilitarian efforts. The written preservation of early French poems, primitive as they may be, was the result of an altogether different sensibility. The choice and the arrangement of the words and the attention paid to the meter and the assonance show that their authors wished to produce esthetic effects through specifically linguistic means. And the result seemed worthy of being written down. Nevertheless, these poems reflect the pastoral concerns of the Church almost as much as the sermons do, and this is why they were preserved. They are, moreover, no freer from the influence of Latin models than they are from the influence of the Church. They are not transcriptions of the popular songs whose lewd contents and provocative renderings, usually by women, had long been stigmatized by ecclesiastical councils and sermons. Nor are they reproductions of the pious, albeit barbarian, songs with which the *rustici* honored Saint Foy at Conques. They are transpositions of Latin religious poems into French.

This is the case for the oldest of them, the *Séquence de sainte Eulalie* (*Sequence of Saint Eulalie*, c. 881–882). In the Valenciennes manuscript preserving this short piece of twenty-nine lines, it follows another poem, in Latin, in honor of the same saint. Its role was to introduce to the faithful the saint whose feast was celebrated in the day's liturgy. This pedagogical role is evident in the differences distinguishing it from the Latin poem. The latter is a sort of rhetorical commendation of the saint which assumes that her life is already familiar to the listener, whereas the *Séquence* recounts briefly the story of her martyrdom. But both pieces were intended for insertion in the day's liturgy. Both are sequences, poems destined to be sung between, and to the same melody as, an *Alleluia* and its repetition. The rhymes on *-ia* at the beginning and end of the French poem, as well as its place in the manuscript, confirm that it was composed for this purpose. The oldest monument of French literature is thus not simply a religious poem, but a liturgical poem, inserted in the poetic development of the service; a sort of vernacular variant of a Latin poem.

These traits are to be found in all the French poems preserved from the end of the ninth century to the end of the eleventh. However, their liturgical role diminished somewhat during this period. The poems grew longer and were divided into stanzas, and thus escaped from the confines of the sequence; but they were still closely linked to ecclesiastical celebrations. This is true of the tenth-century *Vie de saint Léger* (*Life of Saint Léger*) and the *Passion du Christ* or *Passion du Clermont* (*Passion of Christ* or *Passion of Clermont*) from the end of the same century, which are both contained in a single manuscript at Clermont-Ferrand where the melody is also transcribed. Both poems could easily have been integrated into the liturgy, the *Vie* on the day of the saint's feast, the *Passion* on Palm Sunday or during Holy Week, but both could also have been sung on the same occasions by jongleurs—those singers of saints' lives who escaped Thomas Cabham's condemnation—performing on their own account. This possibility is suggested by the *Chanson de sainte Foy d'Agen* (*Song of Saint Foy of Agen*)—again this little saint of Conques!—an admirable Provençal poem of the second third of the eleventh century. The song, one reads in line 14, is "bella 'n tresca" ("good for a *tresque*"). Ordinarily the word *tresque* meant a sort of farandole, a circle dance of Provençal origin; here, however, it undoubtedly meant that the song was intended to accompany a procession in honor of the saint and could therefore have a para-liturgical function. In the manuscript, moreover, it is placed next to a service for Saint Foy. It is in no way a liturgical poem, however. It is too long (593 lines) and the poem itself mentions that it was sung by a jongleur. This jongleur marked the distance separating him from the Latin, clerical world, moreover, by claiming that that world was the source of his poem: he had heard a Latin book read (lines 1–2); he had heard the song sung by *gramadis*—clerks and men of letters (lines 27–28). He sought to earn the good will of his public and seems to have expected some remuneration.

One observes the same development, the same growing

outwards from the liturgy, in the domain of religious theater. Liturgical dramas were dramatic and musical paraphrases of the lives of saints and of episodes from the Bible, composed and performed in monasteries and their schools to enhance the solemnity of the day. They were composed initially in Latin, of course, but the vernacular language eventually made its appearance in the four French stanzas and the French refrain of the *Sponsus (Bridegroom)*, an eleventh-century portrayal of the parable of the wise and foolish virgins.

Although a secular Latin literature existed at this time, there is no trace of a secular vernacular literature during this entire period, with one tiny and bizarre exception: the tenth-century poem known as the *Aube bilingue de Fleury (Bilingual Dawn Song of Fleury)*. The monastery of Fleury, today Saint-Benoît-sur-Loire, was a very important intellectual center at this time and a focal point of liturgical drama. An *aube*, as we will see later, is a poem evoking the painful separation of lovers in the morning. This one is in Latin, but each stanza is followed by a two-line refrain in the vernacular language. But which vernacular language? This has never been established with any certainty, nor have these two lines ever been truly understood, although dozens of translations have been proposed, some having no points in common. The reason for this, Paul Zumthor has recently suggested, is that these lines really have no meaning.[1] A few of the key words common to all *aubes*—the cry of the watchman, the tears—stand out in isolation, easily recognizable, from a pidgin that sounds like the vernacular language but doesn't mean anything. The hypothesis is daring and seductive. In any event (and paradoxically, if Zumthor's hypothesis is correct) the *aube* of Fleury is the only evidence that at so early a date clerks could be inspired by, and take an interest in, a vernacular poetry that was more than a simple transposition of their own poetry and not subject to their control. It is possible that the refrain is nothing more than a phonetic imitation of a language the poet had not yet assimilated and mastered, or pretended not yet to have assimilated or mastered in order to

---

[1] P. Zumthor, "Un trompe-l'oeil linguistique? Le Refrain de *L'aube bilingue de Fleury,*" *Romania* 105 (1984): 171–92.

preserve intact its powerful strangeness. Even if it is no more than this, however, the introduction of the vernacular language into the refrain, like a citation, still manifests an interest in vernacular poetry, perhaps even a fascination with it.

This important poem may preserve the written echo of an autonomous poetry in the vernacular language, but it remains an exception. Up until the end of the eleventh century, the general evolution of our first literary texts corresponds to the development outlined above, distancing them slowly, little by little, from the Latin liturgical models from which they derived. This development culminated in the second half of the eleventh century in the Provençal *Boeci* (*Boethius*) and the French *Vie de saint Alexis* (*Life of Saint Alexis*). The *Boeci* is a fragment of a paraphrase of the *De consolatione philosophiae* (*Consolation of Philosophy*), which was written at the end of the fifth century by Boethius while he was in the prison of his master, King Theodoric; it exercised considerable influence in the realms of both literature and philosophy throughout the Middle Ages. The 278 lines of the *Boeci* correspond to fifty lines of its model; if the paraphrase were complete, it would run to almost 30,000 lines. Although Boethius was sometimes considered a saint and a martyr, some of his medieval readers were troubled by the fact that he was so much more a Neo-Platonist than a true Christian. It is thus not surprising that the *Boeci* has no link to liturgy. It does not represent much of a break, however, either with Latinity, insofar as it is a translation, or with the clerical universe, insofar as its model is a philosophical text that played a major role in the intellectual life of the time.

The *Vie de saint Alexis* is perhaps slightly earlier and is much more significant. Of the surviving French poems, it was the longest (625 lines), the most poetically elaborate, and the most technically masterful up to that time. The tone and the style of the soon-to-emerge *chansons de geste* (epic songs) are already apparent in it at certain points, and its stanzas of five decasyllabic, assonant lines anticipate the epic stanza, or *laisse*. The work enjoyed a durable success that was not entirely eclipsed by the subsequent development of French literature. It is found in five manuscripts copied between the twelfth and fourteenth centuries. It was after hearing a jongleur recite the *Vie* in 1174 that Pierre Waldes, a rich citizen of Lyon, distributed his goods to the poor and began to preach evangelical poverty. He was a precursor of Saint Francis of Assisi, albeit an unfortunate one since he was rejected by the Church and became, in spite of himself, the eponymous founder of the Waldensian sect. The *Vie de saint Alexis* testifies to the elaborateness and literary qualities French religious literature could henceforth attain. The rest of this book will be devoted principally to secular literature; but it is important to remember that this religious literature remained extremely abundant throughout the Middle Ages in the form of saints' lives, miracle stories, prayers in verse, edifying treatises, and so on. But it remained fundamentally a transposition of a Latin literature into French, as is exemplified by the *Vie de saint Alexis*, an adaptation of a Latin life of this saint, itself translated from a Greek life that was inspired, in turn, by a Syriac text. The first French literary texts are the fruit of an apologetic, pastoral, missionary movement that could not by itself give birth to a truly original literature. If French literature had known only this first birth, it would have vegetated in the shadow of Latin letters. But in the last years of the eleventh century a second birth took place, more sudden than the first, more surprising, and more promising.

3 *The* Chansons de Geste

Two very different literary forms appeared more or less simultaneously in the last years of the eleventh century. Both broke neatly with the models offered by Latin literature, and for a time they constituted the essential manifestations of French literature: the *chanson de geste* (epic song) in the language of *oïl* and the lyric poetry of the troubadours in the language of *oc*. The oldest known *chanson de geste*, the version of the *Chanson de Roland* (*Song of Roland*) preserved in the Oxford manuscript, undoubtedly dates from around 1098; and the first troubadour, William IX, count of Poitiers and duke of Aquitaine, lived from 1071 to 1127.

Definition and Nature of the Genre
Chansons de geste are epic poems. They would thus seem to confirm the rule that the epic poem is always one of the first manifestations of a literary tradition—if the uniquely medieval dialectic of innovation and continuity did not once again complicate matters. They are sung narrative poems, as their name suggests (*chanson* = song), and treat of past high deeds, as their name also indicates. The word *geste* corresponds in effect to a nominative feminine singular *gesta*, substituted for the neuter plural *gesta* (things done, high deeds, exploits), from the past participle of *gero*.

These poems are defined by a particular form and content. First, the form: they are composed of homophonic, assonant, *laisses* (stanzas of irregular length). The meter is decasyllabic with an *a minori*, or minor, caesura (a caesura after the fourth syllable) or, less often, an *a maiori*, or major, caesura (after the sixth syllable). Towards the end of the twelfth century, the decasyllable found a rival in the then fashionable alexandrine (a twelve-syllable line, usually with a caesura after the sixth syllable), but the decasyllable was still felt to be the epic meter par excellence even in the sixteenth century when Ronsard, for example, chose to write his *Franciade* in decasyllables. As was noted above, the *Vie de Saint Alexis* (*Life of Saint Alexis*) was written in homophonic, assonant decasyllables, but its five-line stanzas are short and regular; the *Chanson de sainte Foy d'Agen* (*Song of Saint Foy of Agen*) was composed in homophonic, assonant *laisses*, but the meter is octosyllabic, the common meter of medieval Latin poetry that became the meter of the romance.

The word *laisse* is itself sufficient to provide us with a preliminary idea of the esthetic system of the *chansons de geste*. Derived from the verb *laissier*, which in turn comes from the vulgar Latin *laxare*, it meant essentially "what one leaves behind" and developed a variety of other meanings based on this essential one, from "bequest" or "donation" to "excrement." In the domain of literature, it generally designated a passage, a paragraph, or a tirade from a text or poem that formed a satisfactory whole, dealt with a single proposition, and could be recited or sung in a single, uninterrupted poetic "flight." The composition of epics in *laisses* thus implies a series of such flights, more separate than connected. One launches oneself in a flight of poetic proliferation, so to speak, then, a moment later, lands, pauses, catches one's breath, and then takes off on a new flight in another assonance, which emphasizes the rupture, as does the ultimate melodic cadence of the *laisse* and the shorter line that sometimes ends it. This is the source of the particular poetic effects that the *chanson de geste* produces and on which it plays. There is no straight, pure narrative line here, as if the desire to know what is going to happen next is not of primary concern. On the contrary, the *chanson* delights in repetitions and echoes and appears to be caught in a perpetual undertow: a succession of repetitive *laisses* differing only in their assonance and the infinitesimal variations in point of view or content produced by the technique of creating "parallel *laisses*"; an incessant taking up of formulas that are half a line, or sometimes a whole line, long; the effect of refrains like the famous "Halt sunt li pui ..." ("High are the mountains ...") of the *Chanson de Roland*; the effect of symmetry like that (also in the *Chanson de Roland*) created by the designation of Ganelon as ambassador, then of Roland as leader of the rear guard, or that born of Charlemagne's successive and opposing rejections of those who volunteer to serve as ambassador.

The *chanson de geste* thus makes use of what one might term the physical effects of language—the almost hypnotic fascination exerted by repetition; the dizziness produced by the same assonance resonating line after line throughout the entire *laisse*, and that produced by a very simple melody, a repeated chant, always the same line after line. These melodies have not in fact come down to us, but our very ignorance confirms their simplicity and stereotypic character: it was pointless to write them down. And we can form some idea of them through indirect testimonies like a line from a parodic *chanson de geste* preserved in the *Jeu de Robin et de Marion* (*Play of Robin and Marion*) and the melodies of certain *chansons de toile* (sewing songs), about which I will say more later. These quasi-physical effects are enhanced by the unique style of the *chansons de geste*: short, sharp sentences, often limited to a single line, joined to the simultaneously regular and unequal hammering of the decasyllable and its asymmetric half-lines; a taste for parataxis and a horror of subordination. Indeed, it seems that the medieval public enjoyed the *chansons de geste* not only for the stories they told, but also for the affective impression they produced since, according to the testimony offered by two romances of the beginning of the thirteenth century, people enjoyed hearing brief fragments of them sung, a single *laisse*, for example, taken out of its context.

The other characteristic trait of the *chansons de geste* is their content. It is the most visible trait and the one that was initially the most striking to modern readers. They are mainly about warfare, and the events they relate have the peculiarity of always taking place during the Carolingian period, usually during the reign of Charlemagne or his son Louis the Pious. The poems' characters are Charlemagne's barons, who fight the Saracens or defend their rights against the emperor or his weak son. They are grouped into three principal cycles, each organized around a character or a lineage: the *geste* of the king, whose kernel is the *Chanson de Roland*; the *geste* of the rebellious barons, with Doon of Mayence and Ogier the Dane; and the *geste* of Garin of Monglane, whose main hero is William of Orange. Spinning off from a first epic poem containing a striking episode or a crucial theme, like the *Chanson de Roland* or the *Chanson de Guillaume* (*Song of William*), subsequent poems either went further back in time and recounted the youth and first exploits of the hero, the history of his father, then that of his grandfather, and so on, or continued on from the first poem and described the hero's old age, like the *Moniage Guillaume* (*William's Monkhood*), or the lives of his descendants.

While the *chansons de geste* all situate the actions they describe during the Carolingian period, the oldest to come down to us dates, in the state in which we have it, to the very end of the eleventh century. Why should these poems have systematically described events that had occurred—or were supposed to have occurred—three centuries earlier? Or were the *chansons de geste* composed during the Carolingian period, at roughly the same time as the events they relate, even though we can first grasp them only at that moment when they were finally written down, after being transmitted orally for centuries? For more than a century, these questions have been answered in contradictory ways and have provoked an often heated debate. Before summarizing this debate and pointing out its implications and consequences (beyond the traditional and insoluble question of the origin of the genre), I will try to approach it through a concrete case that is also the oldest, the most illustrious, and the most interesting of them all, that of the *Chanson de Roland*.

The Example of the *Chanson de Roland*

The *Chanson de Roland* tells the story of how, on the way back to France from a victorious seven-year expedition in Spain, the rear guard of Charlemagne's army, commanded by his nephew Roland who is accompanied by the twelve peers, is attacked by Saracens at Roncesvalles as a result of the treason of Ganelon, Roland's stepfather. The hero and all his companions are killed in the battle, but their deaths are avenged by the emperor.

The poem, whose renown makes this brief résumé superfluous, has been preserved in six manuscripts, not counting those containing only short fragments of it. The same poem is contained in all the manuscripts, and yet there are no two lines that are truly identical from one version to the others. In some, the poem is written in decasyllables, in others, alexandrines—in yet other cases it changes from one to the other in the course of the poem, just as some versions change from assonance to rhyme. Even the length of the texts varies from 4,000 lines in the oldest manuscript to almost 9,000 lines in one of the more recent ones (from the end of the thirteenth century). These variations provide interesting hints concerning the transmission and evolution of *chansons de geste*, but they also argue in favor of studying the oldest version—the so-called "O" version contained in manuscript Digby 23 of the Bodleian Library at Oxford—separately from the others. This has been done often, and the Oxford version also seems to me to be the most gripping. It is this one that is meant, therefore, when the *Chanson de Roland* is referred to in the following paragraphs.

The O version was probably composed around 1100. Numerous indications converge on this date and prove that it cannot have been composed much earlier: the language of the poem, for example, certain details that seem to echo the First Crusade, or the mention of drums and camels, whose use had frightened the Christians at the battle of Zalaca in 1086. Nor can it have been composed much after 1100 because it was extremely popular during the first years of the twelfth century (but perhaps an earlier version existed). It was composed around 1100, then, but the event providing its subject, the battle of Roncesvalles, had taken place on 15 August 778. These are the terms in which the enigma of the *chansons de geste* is couched in the case of the *Chanson de Roland*.

What do we know about this event? The *Royal Frankish Annals* mention a victorious expedition into Spain by Charlemagne in the year 778, but they say nothing of any defeat. However, another version of the annals written about twenty years later adds that during the trip back from Spain many Frankish leaders were killed in an ambush by Basques, who pillaged the army's baggage before fleeing. None of the victims is named. Written around 830, Einhard's *Vita Caroli magni* (*Life of Charlemagne*) reports that in crossing the Pyrenees the emperor experienced "something of the Basques' perfidy" and adds that "in this battle were killed the Seneschal Eggihard, Anselm, count of the palace, and Roland, prefect of the Breton March, among many others." Eggihard's epitaph, preserved elsewhere, specifies that he died 15 August, thus indicating the exact day of the battle. Ten years later, finally, the author of the *Vita*

Hludovici imperatoris (*Life of Louis the Emperor*), who is known as the Limousine Astronomer, recorded frustratingly that "those who were marching in the rear guard of the army were massacred in the mountains; since their names are well known, I will not repeat them here."

These accounts lead to three conclusions. First, far from being forgotten little by little, the event was mentioned more and more insistently as time went by, until it had become so well known that such insistence was no longer necessary. Second, Einhard indeed names Roland, but last, and his name is not in all the manuscripts of the *Vita*. Roland was, in his eyes, the least important of the three illustrious men who had died in the battle. We also know nothing about Roland, whereas both the Seneschal Egginhard and the Palatine Count Anselm are known to us from other sources. Third, all the texts agree that the ambush was the work of Basques. Although it confirms the growing, and surprising, celebrity of the battle of Roncesvalles, then, the *Chanson de Roland* also appears to have modified history in two fundamental ways, giving Roland an importance he never had—supposing that he ever existed—and substituting Saracens for the Basques.

Arab historians give a somewhat different version of the facts, however. According to Ibn Al-Athir (thirteenth century), Charlemagne entered Spain at the invitation of the governor of Saragossa, Sulayman Ben Al-Arabi, who was in revolt against the Umayyad caliph of Cordoba. But when he came to Saragossa, he found the doors of the city closed to him as a result of a change of heart on the part of Ben Al-Arabi. Having succeeded in capturing the governor, the emperor left for France, taking Ben Al-Arabi with him as a prisoner. While he was traveling through the pass of Ibañeta (Roncesvalles), the sons of Ben Al-Arabi, supported undoubtedly by Basques, attacked the Franks and freed their father. According to Ibn Al-Athir, then, the battle of Roncesvalles was not a simple run-in between the French and some mountain men who wanted to loot the baggage, but a fight between French and Saracens. It was also a rather serious loss for Charlemagne.

This version of the events is corroborated and made plausible in various ways. It agrees in certain details with the Latin *Annals*, which mention, for example, the capture of Ben Al-Arabi, but say nothing at all about him subsequently, and this in circumstances in which such a hostage would have been most useful to Charlemagne. If Ibn Al-Athir's version is right, or close to right, it gives a new meaning to the writings of the Latin historiographers and explains perfectly the growing attention given to the defeat. Written soon after the defeat, the official *Annals* would thus seem to have tried to pass over it in silence. But it was so widely known, and had made such an impression that in future years it became impossible not to mention it at least in passing, minimizing its importance at the price of a certain incoherence in the details that permits one to guess at the truth. A looters' raid on the baggage? Really? So what were people like the seneschal—a sort of commander of the general staff—and the count of the palace—a sort of commander of Charlemagne's personal guard—doing in the middle of the baggage train?

All this remains hypothetical. If it were true, however, the long memory that, three centuries later, surfaced in the French poem would be right and the official history would be wrong— at least insofar as the nature of the battle is concerned, for all the rest is clearly pure fiction. The historical existence of Roland remains an enigma, and other characters are surely legendary.

But doesn't this long memory provide some insight into the past? Can one make the "silence of the centuries" speak, as Bédier put it? Can one discover the trace of a legend of Roland that existed before the *Chanson de Roland*, or even a *Chanson de Roland* that existed before the O version? Scholars have long observed that certain traits of the existing *Chanson* are too archaic for the end of the eleventh century: for instance, the bow Charlemagne solemnly gives to Roland before the battle as a sign of the delegation of command; or the borders of France in the *Chanson*, which are those of the Carolingian France of Charles the Simple, not those of the France of the first Capetians. At the beginning of the twelfth century (thus after the Oxford *Roland*, a fact that impugns somewhat his testimony) the historian William of Malmesbury affirmed that at the battle of Hastings in 1066, a jongleur intoned the *cantilena Rolandi* (*Song of Roland*) to encourage the Normans. Other indirect testimony likewise suggests the existence of epic poetry in

French at an early date: at the end of the ninth century, the Monk of Saint Gall alluded to the stories of old soldiers, and the Poeta Saxo mentioned panegyrics of great men in the vernacular language; Latin texts like the "Hague fragment" (between 980 and 1030) and the *Waltharius* (ninth or tenth century) seem to fore-echo the *chansons de geste*. Above all, the *Nota Emilianense*, copied around 1065–1070 in a Spanish manuscript—thirty or forty years before the Oxford poem—summarizes the story of the *Chanson de Roland* and mentions—side by side with Roland, Oliver, Bishop Turpin, and Ogier—William *alcorbitunas*, "William with the Curved (*courbe*) Nose," before he became "William with the Short (*court*) Nose," the William of Orange of the later *chansons de geste*. Finally, in charters from throughout the eleventh century, from Anjou to Béarn, from Auvergne to Provence, one finds brothers named Oliver and Roland; and, enigmatically, Oliver is always the elder brother, Roland the younger.

Evidence thus exists for a *Roland* composed between the battle of Roncesvalles and the Oxford poem, a *Roland* earlier than the *Chanson de Roland*. But how should this evidence be interpreted? This question is at the center of the debate on the origins of the *chanson de geste*.

The Question of Origins
This is the first question medievalists asked in the nineteenth century because they were influenced by the ideas of romanticism, and in particular by those of Herder and the brothers Grimm, concerning the collective soul and the national genius of a people, which manifested themselves, supposedly, at the beginning of its history and its culture by means of spontaneous, anonymous artistic productions. By bringing the origins of the *chansons de geste* to light, it seemed, one would also illumine the French national identity. This is the spirit in which Gaston Paris first elaborated, in 1865, the theory of the *cantilènes*. After the great invasions, according to Paris, a new national consciousness emerged little by little by means of a poetic activity that reflected the sentiments of the new nation. This poetry, lyric in form, epic in content, took the form of *cantilènes*, short

narrative songs, on historical events.[1] At this time in the nineteenth century, the Homeric poems were thought to be a collection of short, popular pieces that had been brought together
long after their composition to create an apparently coherent,
long epic poem. In the same way, Gaston Paris imagined that
short *cantilènes* had been sewn together to create the *chansons de
geste*. In 1884, however, the Italian Pio Rajna observed, first,
that there is nothing popular about the *chansons de geste*, that,
on the contrary, they exalt the warrior aristocracy; and, second,
that no *cantilène* is known to have existed, and very probably
none ever did.[2] Germanic epics, on the other hand, did indeed
exist during the Carolingian period. To Rajna, the supposed
existence of Romance *cantilènes* served only to mask what the
French *chansons de geste* owed to the Germanic epics. In 1888,
Gaston Paris was won over by Rajna's views,[3] but for a long
time thereafter, during this period of Franco-German rivalry
and conflict, the debate was influenced by political consider-
ations: if one dated the composition of the *chansons de geste* to
the Carolingian period, they were of Germanic origin; if one
considered them to be a creation of the eleventh century, they
formed a purely French genre.

This second attitude is associated above all with Joseph
Bédier, who published his four-volume *Légendes épiques* between
1908 and 1913.[4] For him, the *chansons de geste* were based on
poetic themes rather than on historical memories. Far from
being the product of a slow process of creation and the fruit of
a tradition, they were created all at once by poets who were
perfectly conscious of their art. The most original aspect of his
theory, however, is evident in the first words of his work: "In
the beginning was the road, marked out by sanctuaries. Before
the *chanson de geste*, the legend: a local legend, a church legend." Along the pilgrimage routes, sanctuaries and monasteries
displayed the relics of heroes and martyrs who were liable to

[1] G. Paris, *Histoire poétique de Charlemagne* (Paris: Franck, 1865).

[2] P. Rajna, *Le origini dell'epopea francese* (Florence: Sansoni, 1884).

[3] G. Paris, *La Littérature française au moyen âge: XIᵉ–IVᵉ siècle* (Paris:
Hachette, 1888).

[4] J. Bédier, *Les Légendes épiques*, 4 vols. (Paris: Champion, 1908–13).

attract pilgrims. The *Chanson de Roland* itself attests (*laisse* 267) that one could see the horn of Roland at Saint-Seurin in Bordeaux, his tomb at Blaye. An inspired poet was all that was needed to collect and give life to these stories dispersed along the roads leading to Santiago de Compostela or, in the case of other *chansons de geste*, to Rome. Philipp-August Becker had already proposed this idea twice, in 1896 and in 1907. In developing it and demonstrating it more fully, Bédier added that these stories were the products of a deliberate propaganda effort on the part of the clerks to enhance the reputation of their sanctuaries. The clerks, at Bordeaux and Blaye, for example, had read the story of Roland's death in Einhard's *Vita Caroli magni* (*Life of Charlemagne*). They then invented the history of the Rolandian relics in order to show them to pilgrims and thus publicize their churches. They slipped this story to some poet and gave him the documents he needed to make good use of it. On the basis of what they had told him, he wrote the entire *Chanson de Roland*. In the same way, as a result of their rivalry with the monks of Aniane, the monks of Gellone—today Saint-Guilhem-le-Désert—exploited the legend of their bellicose founder, bringing William of Orange to the attention of poets. The clerks of Vézelay and of Pothières did the same with Girart of Roussillon, and so on. According to Bédier, there were no *chansons de geste* before the end of the eleventh century. If a *Chanson de Roland* existed before the one we know, it was only a rough draft. The Oxford *Roland*, for Bédier, was the creation of one person. It was written from one end to the other by Turold, its enigmatic signatory, three centuries after the fight at Roncesvalles, without any poetic intermediary between the fight and the composition of the *Chanson*. All the other *chansons de geste* were, in the same way, born of "church legends." And Bédier concluded:

> One should speak no longer of epic songs from the time of Charlemagne or of Clovis, nor of a popular, spontaneous, anonymous poetry born of events, gushing from the soul of a whole people; it is time to replace the mystic

heritage of the Grimms with other, more concrete, notions, with other, more explicit, explanations.[1]

Supported by the uncommon talents of its author, Bédier's theory was widely accepted for many decades. But it was elaborated at a time when the "silence of the centuries" had not yet spoken and no one knew, for example, of all the pairs of brothers named Oliver and Roland or of the *Nota Emilianense*. And it bordered on the paradoxical by its extreme downplaying of the existence of an oral poetry prior to the earliest known texts, while inviting less skillful zealots to deny the existence of such a poetry altogether. In the 1920s, Ferdinand Lot responded to Bédier's so-called "individualism" by defending the "traditionalist" position and maintaining that the *chansons de geste* preceded and created the cult of epic heroes linked to sanctuaries on the pilgrimage routes rather than succeeding, and being produced by, it:

> I accept that all the *chansons* of the William cycle may be explained by the Regordanian Way, by Gellone, etc.— except for one, the oldest, the ancestor, the *Chanson de Guillaume*.
> I accept that all the *chansons* whose action is set in Spain know—and admirably well—the road leading to Compostela, except one, the oldest, the *Chanson de Roland*, which knows nothing about the way to Santiago.[2]

If church legends are not the origin of the *chansons de geste*, "there is no option but to return to the old theory of the transmission from century to century." Thus *Gormont et Isembart* (*Gormont and Isembart*), going back to Louis III's victory over the Normans in 881, was not developed from monastic annals, but was, rather, an adaptation of a Norman version of the poem that made its way to the continent in the ninth or the tenth century. *Girart de Vienne* (*Girart of Vienne*) was based on the *chanson* of a jongleur contemporary with the events at Vienne in

---

[1] J. Bédier, *Les Légendes épiques*.
[2] F. Lot, "Etudes sur les légendes épiques françaises IV: Le Cycle de Guillaume d'Orange," *Romania* 53 (1927): 449–73.

870–871. *Raoul de Cambrai* (*Raoul of Cambrai*) actually derived, as the text itself maintains, from the poem of a certain Bertolai who fought at the battle of Origny in 943. The traditionalist thesis was maintained above all, and with unflagging vigor, by Ramón Menéndez Pidál.[1] Reacting to Bédier and his disciples, who argued that the "supreme excellence" of the O version of the *Chanson de Roland* was a reason to believe that it was the original creation of a single, inspired poet, Pidál felt obliged, wrongly, to denigrate the admirable Oxford version in favor of other versions, especially the V4 version (the first Venice version). But over and above this polemical detail and his somewhat fussy efforts to establish the historical value of the *chansons de geste*, Pidál's thinking was based entirely on one essential idea whose fertility will soon become clear. This was the idea that the medieval text was not born from the imagination or the pen of its author in a definitive, perfect, and unchangeable state; the text lived, rather, through its variants, and thanks to them, it transformed itself and constantly brought itself up to date, generation after generation. There was no authentic and correct text that has been corrupted by the mistakes of successive copies; each version of a text corresponds to a moment of its life and thus enjoys a dignity and an interest equal to those of every other version— even if they are not all equal in esthetic value and the felicities of inspiration. In the case of the *chansons de geste*, every version reflects a performance. Although it grew out of the somewhat old-fashioned discussion about origins—but Pidál was over ninety when he wrote the book mentioned above!—this approach places the complex relation between speaking and writing discussed in Chapter One at the center of the debate.

From the Oral Performance to Its Written Trace
As we have seen, the *chansons de geste* themselves imply that they were diffused orally by jongleurs. The prologues and certain comments made by the narrators in the course of the

[1] R. Menéndez Pidál, *La Chanson de Roland y el neotradicionalismo (orígenes de la épica románica)* (Madrid: Espasa-Calpe, 1959). French trans., I.-M. Cluzel, *La Chanson de Roland et la tradition épique des Francs* (Paris: Picard, 1960).

texts make this very clear. The importance of variant readings, brought to light by Pidál, likewise suggests this type of diffusion. The combination of these two observations permits us to explain simultaneously the evolution of the texts, their points of disagreement, their fundamental stability and perpetual renewal, their profound permanence over the centuries despite their superficial variations, and their endurance. All the same, by affirming that the *chanson de geste* "lives through its variants," Pidál meant only that the slight changes made by each performer kept the *chanson* in a state of continuous re-elaboration. Others, like the Swiss Jean Rychner[1] and, above all, the American Joseph Duggan,[2] who applies to the *chanson de geste* the theories of his countrymen Milman Parry and Albert Lord,[3] go further. They consider each performance to be a new creation of a poem that does not truly exist in and of itself, independent of its performance. For them, in effect, the performance is not based ultimately on a memorization of the poem—a memorization whose imperfection is reflected in the variants. Using the example of the modern Yugoslavian singers of epics, Lord showed that the singer, by means of formulaic phrases containing the typical actions of the epic plot, learns to re-create the long verse narratives of the oral tradition extemporaneously each time he performs the poem. According to Duggan, the formulaic style characteristic of the *chansons de geste* reveals their oral character. He even refuses to attribute the Oxford *Roland* to a talented writer who revised a pre-existing oral tradition because, he observes, the crucial episodes often taken to be evidence of the poem's composition by a single, gifted author— the episode of the embassy, that of the horn—conform more closely to the formulaic style than do the others. In his opinion, if two distinct narrative genres, the *chanson de geste* and the romance, existed in twelfth-century France, it was simply because the one was oral and the other written. And in order to

---

[1] J. Rychner, *La Chanson de geste: Essai sur l'art épique des jongleurs* (Geneva: Droz, 1955).

[2] J. Duggan, *The Song of Roland: Formulaic Style and Poetic Craft* (Berkeley: Univ. of California Press, 1973).

[3] M. Parry, *The Making of Homeric Verse* (Oxford: Clarendon, 1970); A. Lord, *The Singer of Tales* (Cambridge, Mass.: Harvard Univ. Press, 1960).

demonstrate that written *chansons de geste* tended to become like romances, he points out that the formulaic style is less pronounced in *Beuves de Commarchis* (*Beuves of Commarchis*), a late *chanson de geste* from around 1270 by Adenet le Roi, than it is in the *Siège de Barbastre* (*Siege of Barbastre*), which is a century older than Adenet's poem and served as its model.

In reality, however, the formulaic style is found everywhere and is in no way unique to oral literature. It does not in itself constitute proof of orality, and both Lord's theory and Duggan's application of it seem too rigid. As we saw in the first chapter, the opposition between the oral and the written, rarely absolute anywhere or at any time, is never absolute in the Middle Ages. Poets, too, were conscious of this opposition and ceased to evolve in a world of absolute orality from the moment they had access to the two modes of expression. The style they adopted, the effects they produced, and the techniques they used were all "artificial." They were the products of deliberate, at least partially conscious decisions, and cannot be interpreted unequivocally. After all, the *chansons de geste* are known to us only in written form even though they were diffused and circulated orally. The elements that theoretically belong to oral creation, like the formulaic style, are preserved in a written text. The indications of oral enunciation—an appeal to the audience, a request for silence, an announcement that the performer is going to break off in order to pass the hat, to rest, or to get a drink—were carefully recopied in the silence of the *scriptorium*. The artifice is patent.

Of course this artifice may be nothing more than a simple historical discrepancy due to fixed habits and the fundamental conservatism of human behavior. Even if the form and the stylistic characteristics of the poem were conceived for oral performance, they could have survived for a long time without any function in the written poem. Moreover, as Duggan remarks, they grew less pronounced over time. But one may also suppose that a sense of historical discrepancy was, from a very early date, a part of the esthetic system of the *chansons de geste*. From the moment they were written down, they were pleasing because they were stiff and familiarly "archaic," because the stylistic and formal effects linked to their orality made them distant, even when this orality became fictitious. Seen in this

[handwritten margin note: Z.]

[handwritten margin note: cf. record "albums"]

[handwritten margin note: the Bible ?!]

light, the strongly formulaic style of certain bravura passages is an indication less of orality than of a deliberate recourse, at important moments, to the characteristic stylistic effect of the genre. A similar impulse may be seen rather clearly in certain *chansons de geste* that resisted the temptation of rhyme, obstinately and with obvious effort, long after assonance had ceased to be anything more than a curiosity. The *chansons de toile* (sewing songs), which will be discussed later, cultivated the stiff archaism of the epic form in a similar way.

The Evolution of the *Chansons de Geste*
The interest that the appearance and the prehistory of the *chansons de geste* legitimately provoke should not obscure the fact that the genre remained alive throughout the Middle Ages and that all in all it evolved little during this time. The poems did become longer, however, the plots more complex, and, above all, they gave an ever greater role to love and the marvelous. The thirteenth-century *Huon de Bordeaux* (*Huon of Bordeaux*) is a good example of this evolution. The *chansons de geste* thus grew to be more like romances. At the end of the thirteenth and beginning of the fourteenth century, a number of hybrid works appeared that poured themselves into the epic mold of the homophonic *laisse*—in alexandrines more often than in decasyllables—but whose content was drawn from both genres, and sometimes predominantly from romance (*Berthe au grand pied* [*Big-Foot Berthe*] by Adenet le Roi, *Florence de Rome* [*Florence of Rome*], *La Belle Hélène de Constantinople* [*Beautiful Helen of Constantinople*], *Brun de la Montagne* [*Brun of the Mountain*]). As we will see later, the rise of prose at the end of the Middle Ages completed the fusion of the two genres.

But before that, during the heyday of the *chanson de geste* at the end of the twelfth century, the crusades provided the genre with a new, contemporary subject. Modeled on traditional *chansons de geste* on Carolingian topics, a new crusade cycle appeared (*La chanson d'Antioche* [*The Song of Antioch*], *Les captifs* [*The Captives*], *La prise de Jérusalem* [*The Capture of Jerusalem*]) and was kept alive to the very end of the Middle Ages by means of continuations, the joining together of existing poems, and numerous reworkings of the legend of the *Chevalier du Cygne* (Knight of the Swan) and of Godefroy de Bouillon.

The *chanson de geste* is thus more than just one of the oldest forms of French literature. It remained the privileged mode of expression for military exploits and Christian warfare throughout the Middle Ages.

4   *Troubadours and Trouvères*

A Paradoxical Appearance
Indirect evidence indicates that songs circulated in lay society well before the Romance languages were formed, especially love songs sung by women which particularly troubled the Church. But in creating a liturgical poetry the Church itself abandoned the traditional rhythm of alternating long and short syllables that formed the foundation of classical Latin versification and, taking its inspiration from these popular rhythms, based its meter instead on numbers of feet and rhyme. The first complete extant lyric poems in the vernacular language—in Provençal as it turns out—have nothing "popular" about them, however, regardless of the precise meaning one wishes to give to that word. They are complex, refined, deliberately obscure. They are desperately aristocratic and elitist, advertising with a provocative arrogance their contempt for such bumpkins as are unable to appreciate them and insensitive to elegance of manners and spirit. And the first poet whose work has come down to us was one of the most powerful princes of his time, William IX, count of Poitiers and duke of Aquitaine (1071–1127). Within a few years, his poetic successors and emulators, the troubadours, had multiplied in every southern French court and, in the second half of the twelfth century, they were imitated in the north of France by the trouvères. A court poetry: such was the origin of this *courtly* lyricism whose sudden appearance was as provocative as the conception of love it celebrated.

Courtliness and *fin'amor*
Courtliness and courtly love in no way constituted an autonomous doctrine, conceived and promulgated in a coherent and definitive way. They did indeed find a sort of theorist in the person of Andreas Capellanus (or Andreas the Chaplain), who wrote a *Tractatus de amore* (*Treatise on Love*) around 1184 at the

court of Champagne. But his work was a late codification of practices that had already existed for almost a century and it is difficult to interpret. In reality, all that one can do is to extract empirically from the works of the troubadours a common sensibility and an amorous, worldly ethical system, in full awareness of the fact that this sensibility and this system had no expression other than in the poetry that is their vehicle. It is thus rather artificial, albeit useful and necessary for what follows, to begin this discussion with an inevitably simplified outline of courtliness and courtly love.

The idea of courtliness involved a conception of both life and love. It demanded a nobility of heart (if not of birth), impartiality, liberality, and a good education in all its forms. In order to be courtly one had to know how things were done and how to conduct oneself in company with ease and distinction, to be skilled at hunting and fighting, and to have a spirit sufficiently lively to grasp the refinements of conversation and poetry. In order to be courtly one had to have both a taste for luxury and a detached familiarity with it, and a horror of, and disdain for, any hint of cupidity, avarice, or the desire for gain. Whoever was not courtly was a *vilain*, a word that originally meant "peasant," but quickly took on a moral signification. The *vilain* was greedy, voracious, vulgar. He thought only of amassing and hoarding. He was jealous of everything he possessed or thought he possessed, of his goods, of his wife.

But no one could be perfectly courtly unless he loved, for love multiplied the lover's good qualities and even endowed him with those he lacked. The originality of courtliness lay in the essential role it gave to women and to love. It was original with respect to both the teachings of the Church and the customs of the day. The courtly lover's lady was his *dame*, his *domna* (from the Latin *domina*), which is to say his feudal sovereign. He would do anything she wished; his only desire was to merit the favors she could always freely grant or refuse.

Courtly love, or *fin'amor* (refined love), was founded on the idea that love and desire are the same thing. Desire, by definition, is the desire to be satisfied, but when it is satisfied, of course, it disappears. This is why love simultaneously seeks and dreads the satisfaction that will put an end to desire. Love thus entails a perpetually unresolvable conflict between desire and the desire to desire, between love and the love of love. This is the explanation for the complex emotion unique to love, a mixture of suffering and pleasure, anguish and exaltation. The troubadours had a word for this complex emotion: they called it *joi*, which is not the same as the feminine noun *joya*, the medieval Provençal equivalent of the modern French *joie* or "joy" by which it is usually translated for lack of anything better. Jaufré Rudel, for example, wrote:

> D'aquest amor suy cossiros
> Vellan e pueys somphnan dormen,
> Quar lai ay joy meravelhos.

(I am tormented by this love when I am awake and when, sleeping, I dream: then I have marvelous *joi*.)

This fundamental insight leads to the belief that love should not be satisfied rapidly or easily, that it must first deserve to be satisfied, and that one should multiply the obstacles that will exacerbate the desire before satisfying it. Whence a certain number of requirements all proceeding from the principle that the lady must be, not inaccessible, for courtly love was not Platonic, but difficult of access. This is why, theoretically, love could not exist within marriage, where desire faded because it could always be satisfied, and where the man's right to the woman's body prevented him from thinking of her as his *mistress* in the true sense of the word, whose freely given favors he had to earn. In principle, therefore, one had to love another man's wife. It is thus not surprising that the first quality required of a lover was discretion and that his worst enemies were the *lauzengiers*, the jealous slanderers who spied on him in order to denounce him to the lady's husband. The lady, moreover, was supposed to be of a higher social rank than her suitor so that their amorous relations could be modeled on feudal relations and so that the two partners would not be tempted; she, to grant her favors out of self interest, he, to use his authority over her to force her to give in to him.

One should not exaggerate the importance of these rules, however, which come to the fore only in a specialized genre of love casuistry like the *jeu-parti* (a poetic debate), where they must be taken with a grain of salt, and are ultimately less prominent in the works of the poets themselves than they are in the works of their commentators. They were the most visible consequence of the equation of love with desire, but they were not the essential one. The essential consequence was the peculiar turn this equation gave to the troubadours' eroticism. In their work, there is a mixture of respectful fear and bold sensuality in the presence of the beloved lady that gives their love its adolescent traits: a deliberate tendency towards voyeurism, a taste for erotic dreams, which exhaust desire without satisfying it, a feverish and detailed imagining of the female body and the caresses it invites, along with a refusal to imagine the most intimate part of that body and a repugnance to envisage the consummation of the sexual act. This body, which "will kill [the poet] if he cannot touch it naked," this body "white as the snow of Christmas," "white like the snow after a frost" (these are all Bernard de Ventadour's words), this body is, like snow, burning and icy, or chilling.

The Poetry of the Troubadours
Before they were celebrated in a slightly different spirit by the romances, courtliness and *fin'amor* were promulgated only in the lyric poetry of the troubadours in the language of *oc* and, later, in that of the trouvères in the language of *oïl*, that is, in the work of those who "find" (in Provençal *trobar* means "to find"), or invent, poems. It was a lyric poetry in the true sense of the word, a sung, monodic poetry. Every poet composed, as one of them says, "los moz e'l so" ("the words and the music").

The essential genre of this poetry was the *canso* (song), a term that quickly took over from the earlier *vers* (verse) used by the first troubadours. The *canso*, or *grand chant courtois* (great courtly song) as modern scholars have called it, was a poem of approximately forty to sixty lines divided into stanzas of six to ten lines. It usually ended with a *tornada*, an envoi or short concluding stanza, repeating the melody and the rhymes of the end of the last regular stanza. The metric pattern and the rhyme scheme were often complex and, in principle, original, as was the melody which, beneath a fairly simple melodic line, played intensely with the expressive possibilities of the melismata, the vocal passages sung to single syllables of the text. The rhymes could remain the same from stanza to stanza throughout the entire poem (*coblas unisonans*); they could change every two stanzas (*coblas doblas*); or they could change every stanza (*coblas singulars*). The poets also used *estramp* rhyme, where isolated rhyming words were placed in the same position in two succeeding stanzas. They could rhyme entire words, and use the same rhyme word in the same place in every stanza. The last line of a stanza could be repeated at the beginning of the next stanza. This was a favorite technique of Galician-Portuguese poetry; but the troubadours preferred the technique of identical stanza endings.

But the style and the tone of this poetry are even more striking than its prosodic games. The language is taut, the expression is often willfully complicated, more often elliptic or rocky, with a preference, even in the choice of sounds sometimes, for ruggedness over fluidity. Around the 1170s, certain troubadours cultivated a deliberately hermetic style, or *trobar clus*, a "closed," obscure poetic creation. Raimbaud d'Orange, one of these poets, described his poetic activity in this way:

> Cars, bruns et teinz mots entrebesc,
> Pensius pensanz.

(Precious, dull and brightly colored words, I interlace, thoughtfully thinking.)

Other poets preferred the more accessible "light" or "easy" style of the *trobar leu*. In a debate with Raimbaud d'Orange, for example, Guiraut de Bornelh rejoiced that his songs could be understood by the simple folk at the spring. The *trobar ric*, or "rich" style, finally, was a development of the *trobar clus* whose best representative was Arnaud Daniel. It preferred to play with the sumptuousness of language and words, with virtuosity of versification.

This poetry, so attentive to refined expression, did not seek to be at all original in content. It had no fear of repetition and never tired of saying, song after song, that spring makes one want to sing of love, but that this song is sad in the mouth of one whose love is unrequited. For the troubadours, poetic creation aimed at conforming as closely as possible to an ideal model, while simultaneously introducing tiny transformations and innovations, and rhetorical and metrical subtleties, and playing on the infinite number of ways of combining the conventional motifs. But this "formal" poetics did not constitute, as has sometimes been suggested, a turning inwards upon language itself and an indifference towards the world to which language refers. On the contrary, its monotony and the tautness of its expression seem to have been the consequence of a demand for sincerity that was part of its rules. It presumed that there was an equivalence between the propositions "I love" and "I sing," and from this it deduced that the poet's poem should, in some way, resemble his love, that the characteristics and the perfection of his poem should reflect the characteristics and perfection of his love. As Bernard de Ventadour remarked, he who loved best was also the best poet:

> Non es meravilha s'eu chan
> Melhs de nul autre chantador,
> Que plus me tra'l cors va amor
> E melhs sui failhz a so coman.

(It is no wonder if I sing better than any other singer, for my heart draws me more towards love and I am more obedient to its commands.)

The tensions of the style reflect those of love—of *joi*—and Arnaud Daniel defines himself as both lover and poet in three famous enigmatic lines:

> Eu son Arnauz qu'amas l'aura
> Et chatz la lebre ab lo bou
> E nadi contra suberna.

(I am Arnaud who gathers the wind and hunts the hare with the ox and swims against the tide.)

In general, just as love was supposed to tend towards an ideal perfection without being affected by circumstances and contingencies, so the song that expressed and reflected it was supposed to tend towards an abstract perfection that leaves no room for the anecdotal. It is for this reason that the convention of starting every song with an evocation of spring—a custom that undoubtedly went back to the very roots of Romance lyricism and that produced the brief descriptions of nature that we find so charming—fell out of fashion and was ridiculed in the thirteenth century: the true lover, the trouvères explained again and again, loves in all seasons, not only in the spring.

The Origins

Like that of the *chansons de geste*, albeit for different reasons, the birth of courtly lyricism has received much, sometimes too much, scholarly attention. The characteristics of courtliness and of *fin'amor* and the sophistication of this poetry make it impossible to see it as the simple emergence in writing of a pre-existing *popular* poetry. The fundamental masculinity of the courtly attitude towards love and the submission of the lover to his *dame* are almost sufficient in and of themselves to exclude this possibility. In most civilizations, and, in any event, all around the Mediterranean basin, the oldest love lyrics are attributed to women and look at love from a feminine point of view. As we will see later, all that we can know about the earliest Romance lyricism confirms this general tendency.

Some scholars have suggested that courtly lyricism was simply a transposition into the vernacular language of the courtly Latin poetry that had been practiced in the sixth century by Venantius Fortunatus, bishop of Poitiers, when he praised the noble wives of princes, or, in the eleventh century, by Strabo, Hildebert of Lavardin, and Baudri of Bourgueil—a type of poetry that was also cultivated, at about the same time, by the clerks of the schools of Chartres who sometimes wrote in praise of the townswomen. According to these scholars, those aspects of the troubadours' poetry that go beyond this Platonic exaltation of ladies, and in particular the rather racy songs of the first troubadour, William IX, were the products of the Ovidian inspiration of the goliards, or wandering clerks. It is indeed true that one finds a medieval Latin rhetorical influence and Ovidian echoes in the works of the troubadours. But one has only to read them to understand how much their tone differs from that of Latin poetry, where one finds little of their passionate seriousness that makes love the sum of moral life and, indeed, of life itself. The intellectual centers of Chartres and Angers, moreover, were rather too northern to have played a determining role in the birth of a poetry in the language of *oc*. Apart from the songs of the goliards, furthermore, Latin poetry was read, not sung. Save for certain rare exceptions, finally, the troubadours were far from being well enough versed in Latin culture to carry through this kind of adaptation successfully.

It has been asserted often and for a long time, albeit not without challenges, that courtly poetry and *fin'amor* were of Hispano-Arab origin. Already at the beginning of the tenth century, an Arab poet in Spain like Ibn Da'ud in his *Kitab az-zahrah* (*Book of the Flower*) or, at the beginning of the eleventh century, other Arab poets like Ibn Ḥazm, who wrote his *Ṭawq al-ḥamāma* (*The Dove's Necklace*) around 1020, celebrated an idealized love, called *odhrite* love, that was not altogether unlike *fin'amor*. Beautiful, capricious, and tyrannical women, lovers whose sufferings took the form of true physical illness that could lead to death, confidants, messengers, the threat of guardians and jealous spies, discretion and secrecy, an air of spring: the whole amorous and poetic universe of the troubadours may be found in this literature even though the effects of the differences between the two civilizations are considerable. But the strongest argument in favor of this hypothesis, perhaps rests on the similarity between stanzaic forms in the two poetic traditions. It is not historically impossible that the one influenced the other. The two civilizations were in contact in Spain. The *reconquista* (the reconquest of Moslem Spain by Christian forces) actually encouraged exchanges between the two and we know quite precisely that captive female singers were much appreciated in both camps.

But then why did the poetry of the troubadours flourish to the north and not the south of the Pyrenees? The stanza of the Andalusian *muwashshaḥ* and *zajal*, which the troubadours used later, was unknown to the Arabs until they arrived in Spain. From this, certain scholars concluded that the Arabs borrowed the stanza from the Christian Mozarabs and that the Arab stanza actually imitated an ancient form of Romance lyricism that was later taken up independently by the troubadours. These scholars had two further arguments to support this hypothesis. First, the *kharja*, or ending, of the *muwashshaḥ* is often in the Romance language—and it is thus by the detour of Arab poetry that the oldest fragments of Romance lyricism are known to us. If the Arabs borrowed these citations from the indigenous poetic tradition, they could very well have borrowed its stanzaic forms as well. Second, this type of stanza may be found in Latin liturgical poetry, like the *tropes* of Saint-Martial of Limoges, which was written well before the appearance of the troubadours and had no reason to take its inspiration from erotic Arab poetry.

In truth, neither hypothesis can be proved. Neither, moreover, excludes the other: the play of influences was undoubtedly complicated. Of course, other factors must also be taken into account, like the socio-historical conditions within which this poetry emerged. These include the particular nature of the castle life in which the young nobles did their military and worldly apprenticeship; the hopes and demands of this group of "youths" who, as Georges Duby has pointed out, were excluded for a long time, and sometimes forever, from marriage and its attendant responsibilities (the word "youth" is indeed used with a particular insistence in the poetry of the troubadours);[1] the cultural consequences of the rivalry and mutual imitation between the higher and lower nobility noted by Erich Köhler (although his analysis is more appropriate to the courtly romance than to lyric poetry).[2] All these elements should be considered, so long as they do not become the sources of a simplifying determinism.

From the Troubadours to the Trouvères

Who were the troubadours? Some of them were great lords, like William IX, Dauphin d'Auvergne, Raimbaud d'Orange, or even Jaufré Rudel, "prince of Blaye." Others were petty rural nobles, like Bertrand de Born, Guillaume de Saint-Didier, Raymond de Miraval, or the four castellans of Ussel. Others were poor devils like Cercamon, the second oldest known troubadour, whose nickname means "he who travels the world over," or his disciple Marcabru, a foundling who was first named "Lost Bread,"

[1] G. Duby, "Youth in Aristocratic Society," in *The Chivalrous Society*, trans. C. Postan (Berkeley: Univ. of California Press, 1980), 112–22.

[2] E. Köhler, *Ideal und Wirklichkeit in der höfischen Epik: Studien zur Form der frühen Artus- und Graldichtung*, 2d ed. (Tübingen: Niemeyer, 1970). French trans., E. Kaufholz, *L'aventure chevaleresque: Idéal et réalité dans le roman courtois* (Paris: Gallimard, 1974).

or simply the children of castle servants, like Bernard de Ventadour. Others were clerks. Some of them were unfrocked, like Peire Cardenal who, when he reached his majority, left the "canonry" where he had been sent as a small child in order to become a troubadour; but others were not, like the Monk of Montaudon who supported his monastery on the gifts he received in return for his songs. Others were merchants, like Foulquet de Marseille, who, repenting because he had sung of love, entered a monastery, became abbot of Le Thoronet, then bishop of Toulouse. Others, like Gaucelm Faiditz, were former jongleurs, while others, inversely, were impoverished nobles who became jongleurs like, apparently, Arnaud Daniel. From castle to castle, at this court, around that lady or patron, all these people met one another, exchanged songs, cited and answered one another, argued questions of love and poetry in the poetic dialogues called *jeux-partis*, or abused one another in polemical *sirventès* (satirical or moralizing poems).

How do we know anything about the lives and the characters of the troubadours? The manuscripts that have preserved their songs for us—the *chansonniers*—are one source of information. These are anthologies in which the works of each troubadour are often preceded by a *vida*, or short history of his life, while some songs are accompanied by a *razo*, or commentary, claiming to relate the circumstances of the poem's composition and explain its allusions. Some *vidas* are almost accurate. Others are almost entirely fictitious and based on hints found in the songs themselves. These latter are interesting for what they tell us about the spirit in which the works of the troubadours were read when they were collected, edited, and copied into manuscripts during, or at the end of, the thirteenth century. This thirteenth-century spirit of autobiographical anecdote seems very distant from the generalizing idealization to which the poetry of the troubadours aspired.

Times had changed. Courtliness itself had changed as it had passed to northern France and, at the beginning of the thirteenth century, the northern French imposed this change roughly on the southern courts in the course of the Albigensian crusade.

Courtly lyricism developed in northern France towards the middle of the twelfth century. The symbol, if not the cause, of this expansion was the marriage in 1137 of Eleanor of Aquitaine, the granddaughter of the first troubadour, first, to the king of France, Louis VII the Young, then, after her repudiation in 1152, to the king of England, Henry II Plantagenet. One of the two daughters born of her first marriage, Marie, became the countess of Champagne and the patroness of Andreas Capellanus and, most importantly, of Chrétien de Troyes. The courtly spirit thus reached all the great Francophone courts.

Emulators of the troubadours, the trouvères nonetheless differed from their models in several ways. In the case of the "great courtly song," they were generally more reserved, more prudish even. They used all the resources of versification and rhetoric with deliberate skill, as Roger Dragonetti has shown;[1] but they softened their effects more than the troubadours did and seldom resorted to the harsh, flamboyant, paradoxical, taut style so dear to the southerners. The *trobar clus* style, which even in the south had been no more than a passing fad, was unknown to them. On the other hand, their melodies have survived more often than those of the troubadours, and the last trouvères, like Adam de la Halle in the 1280s, made decisive progress towards polyphony—thus bringing about the ineluctable disintegration of the synthesis of text and music on which courtly lyricism had been founded.

Even the conditions of literary life were different for the trouvères. To be sure, one finds the same social spectrum among the trouvères as among the troubadours. They included princes, like the subtle and fertile Count Thibaud IV de Champagne, king of Navarre; or Jean de Brienne, king of Jerusalem, of whose work only a single *pastourelle* (a song relating an encounter with a shepherdess) survives; and other great lords, or at least eminent figures, like Conon de Béthune or Gace Brulé. But the proportion of noble dilettantes, each writing a few songs because it was part of the social game, was smaller in the north than it was in the south. One sign of this is that even though the overall poetic production of the troubadours and the trouvères was roughly equal, we know the names of about 450

---

[1] R. Dragonetti, *La Technique poétique des trouvères dans la chanson courtoise: Contribution à l'étude de la rhétorique médiévale* (Bruges: De Tempel, 1960).

troubadours but only about 200 trouvères. The greatest difference is that, regardless of the importance of the great literary
courts like that of Champagne, most trouvères belonged to the
literary milieux of the rich commercial towns of the north of
France, especially Arras, from the end of the twelfth century on.

Literary societies that organized poetry competitions appeared in several of these towns in the course of the thirteenth
century. The most illustrious, the *Puy* (poets' association) of
Arras, was associated with a brotherhood named, significantly,
the *Confrérie des jongleurs et bourgeois d'Arras* (Brotherhood of
Jongleurs and Burghers of Arras), and dominated by the greatest commercial families of the town. These urban poets, who
were as likely to be burghers as clerks, continued to compose
"great courtly songs." But, even without falling into the old
error of trying to define a "bourgeois" literature in the thirteenth century, one has to recognize that they had a pronounced taste almost unknown among the troubadours for
those lyric genres that formed a sort of racy, comic counterpoint
to courtliness or seemed to be the heirs of an even older tradition.

This is why I have waited until now to discuss the non-
courtly lyric genres, even though some of them seem to have
descended from the primitive forms of Romance poetry.

The *Chansons de femme* and Non-Courtly Lyricism

There are two sorts of non-courtly genres. One brings us immediately face-to-face with the enigma of a popular poetry, whose
echo these genres preserved or created artificially. These are the
aubes (dawn songs) and the *chansons de toile* (sewing songs).
Elements of popular origin may sometimes be found in the
other genres, and may even play a fundamental role in them,
but these other genres formed, as was said above, the underside
of courtliness and, at least in the state in which they come down
to us, existed only in relation to it: they are the *reverdies* (spring
songs), the *chansons de malmariée* (songs of the mismarried
woman), and the *pastourelles* (songs relating an encounter with
a shepherdess). The *chansons à danser* (dance songs), defined by
their sometimes ancient form, borrowed their themes from all
the other genres, and furnished them in return with refrains
and, occasionally, melodies.

As was mentioned above, the primitive form of amorous lyricism was generally the *chanson de femme*, or "woman's song." Although this primitive poetry is obscured in French literature by the sudden appearance of courtly lyricism, a number of indications testify to its existence: the Church's very early condemnation of lascivious women's songs; the few amorous episodes found in the first *chansons de geste*, like the death of "la belle Aude" ("beautiful Aude") in the *Chanson de Roland*, which seem to reserve for women the elegiac expression of love; and the fact that all the *kharjas* borrowed from Mozarab poetry are taken from women's songs where the singer's love is generally expressed with a passionate and sensual seriousness. The same tone is occasionally recognizable in the poetry of the small number of women troubadours, the *trobairitz*, who usually limited themselves to creating feminine versions of the stereotypes of the "great courtly song."

But above all, there existed in the language of *oïl* an altogether unusual genre, the *chanson de toile* (sewing song), which seems to be related to the tradition of the woman's song, even though the twenty surviving *chansons* were composed long after the development of courtly poetry and have been influenced by it. The form of the *chansons de toile* makes them analogous to little *chansons de geste*. They are almost all in decasyllables. Their stanzas, sometimes rhymed but often assonant, distinguish themselves from epic *laisses* only by their relative brevity, their regularity, and the presence of a refrain. They are narrative songs in the third person. Their style, like that of the *chansons de geste*, is stiff, their syntax avoids subordination, and it is rare that a sentence is longer than a line. They represent young women who are sensually and painfully in love with indolent seducers or distant lovers for whom they wait, seated at a window, busy with their needlework: whence their name. Some of them were inserted in a romance from the beginning of the thirteenth century, Jean Renart's *Roman de la Rose ou de Guillaume de Dole*. This subtle and malicious author, who boasted that he was the first to think of citing lyric pieces in a romance, had the aged widow of a castellan say that "in the old days ladies and queens sang historical songs while making tapestries."

On the basis of this testimony and the existence of the *chansons de toile*, scholars have for a long time accepted without question that these songs were very old. But some of their traits are hard to reconcile with their apparent archaism, which should be interpreted, rather, as either a survival from an earlier stage of the songs, which were otherwise modified, or the product of a conscious effort. What is certain is that the songs we have were written by men. One of them says so, others are the work of a known trouvère, Audefroy le Bastard. It seems that they were fashionable in the refined literary circles of Picardy, Wallonie, and Lorraine during the first third of the thirteenth century, whose members, bored with the sophistication of the "great courtly song," found their simplicity charming. There is thus an element of artifice in their success and, indeed, in their composition; but it is hard to believe that they were entirely made up in these circumstances, and not based on an older tradition.

Other lyric types were more easily bent to the conventions of courtliness. The *chanson d'aube* (dawn song), for example, exists in almost all the poetic traditions of the world, from China to ancient Egypt to Greece. In medieval western Europe, the *aube* was not always a woman's song, but it often was, especially its oldest specimens. Its subject is the painful separation of the lovers the morning after a night of love. It could be integrated easily into the courtly universe since it presupposed clandestine love affairs. In fact, it is the only non-courtly lyric genre whose success was as great, or even greater, among the troubadours as among the trouvères.

Although the remaining non-courtly genres—the *reverdie* (spring song), the *chanson de malmariée* (song of the mismarried woman), the *pastourelle* (song relating an encounter with a shepherdess), and the *rondeau* (round)—were even more clearly adapted to the prevailing poetic fashions, they have sometimes been thought to reveal folkloric sources of French lyricism.

The *reverdie*, as its name suggests (*re* = again, *verdoier* = become green), extended the evocation of spring often found in the initial stanza of the works of the troubadours and trouvères to an entire poem. The few surviving examples thus form a courtly sub-genre. It has been suggested, however, that the *reverdie* surviving residually in the initial spring stanza may echo the celebrations of springtime renewal that, going back to paganism, have persisted in attenuated forms up until almost the present day. These festivals were characterized by a certain license, and during them women could, it is said, take the initiative in love. A charming poem known by the title of the *Ballade de la reine d'avril* (*Ballad of the Queen of April*) has been seen by some as offering explicit testimony that this was the case. But it doesn't appear to be as old as it might at first seem, and it is curiously composed in an artificial language (the language of *oïl* disguised as the language of *oc*), of which, however, it is not the only example.

After the courtly song and the *jeu-parti*, the trouvères' next most favorite genre was the narrative, dialogic song relating an amorous encounter. In it the poet tells how, and with what success, he has tried to seduce a young woman, usually a lady who is unhappy with her husband (the song of the *malmariée* or mismarried woman) or a shepherdess (the *pastourelle*). In these poems, the husband is a *vilain* whose inability to perform his conjugal duties justifies his misfortune, while the surface elegance of the poet's amorous request offers a piquant contrast with both the brutality of his desire and the rusticity of the shepherdess. The whole encounter is thus a pretext for a burlesque and often obscene distortion of the rules of courtliness. To this is added, in the case of the *pastourelles*, the attraction exerted by the shepherdess herself, loaded with all the diffuse eroticism of the reviving nature at whose heart she lives and of which she seems to be an emanation. The phantasms of these songs thus organize themselves around rustic and spring motifs in a sort of spirit of sexual revenge: the revenge of the mismarried woman on her husband, of the young woman on her mother who keeps her from loving, of the knightly skirtlifter on the courtly lady for whom he languishes.

The strength of these phantasms appears in a particularly striking way in the short *rondeaux* (rounds) for dancing deriving, it seems, from a very old stanza form. Pell-mell within the three lines of the stanza and the two lines of the refrain, the authors of these *rondeaux* evoke all the lyric themes in an allusive, fragmentary, dismembered way, knowing full well what secret ties bind their apparent incongruity—the meadow and its new flowers, the young woman at the spring, the shepherdess and her flock, the mismarried woman and her jealous husband, the pain of love and the movements of the dance. Each *rondeau* condenses into five lines this poetry's thin, troubling perfume.

5   *Romance*

A "Secondary" Genre

Romance was secondary neither in terms of its importance nor in terms of its subsequent destiny. But the epithet may be applied to it in two ways. First of all, chronologically: romance appeared towards the middle of the twelfth century, somewhat later than the *chanson de geste* and lyric poetry, so we can see it develop through all its stages, while the other two genres were fully constituted when they first appeared to us. Second, by reason of its character: from the very beginning romance defined itself as a self-reflexive genre, preoccupied by its own processes, and, therefore, as an intellectualized genre.

The *chanson de geste* and the poetry of the troubadours and trouvères were both intended to be sung. Romance was the first medieval literary genre intended to be read. Read aloud, of course, since the custom of individual reading spread only later. But this trait alone sufficed to make it an entirely new form, especially with regard to the *chanson de geste*, the only narrative genre that had preceded it. It renounced the repetitive fascination of the epic melopoiea, the equally repetitive effects of the echo or refrain born of the formulaic style and the technique of parallel *laisses*, and the stanzaic construction that imposed on the listener both its ruptures and its rhythm. For these it substituted the unlimited linearity, without rupture or shock, of octosyllabic couplets, and their erasure or transparency as well. At this time, when literary French prose did not yet exist, the octosyllabic couplet was, and would be for some time, the least marked literary medium, a sort of zero degree of literary writing. It did not seek to play on the emotional, even physical, effects of language and song. It let the audience concentrate on a narrative whose continuity it made no effort to interrupt, permitting the reader to master that narrative, to structure it, to think about it, to understand it. A style and a rhetoric that privileged narration and an appeal to the reader, sometimes explicit, to reflect: these were the two constant traits of the medieval romance.

The First French Romances: From the Matter of Rome to the Matter of Britain

The first French romances were also distinguished from the *chansons de geste* by their subjects. They were adaptations of classical Latin works. The *Roman d'Alexandre* (*Romance of Alexander*), of which there were three versions between 1130 and 1190, is a largely fictional story of the life and conquests of the Macedonian king based on the account of Pseudo-Callisthenes. The *Roman de Thèbes* (*Romance of Thebes*, shortly after 1155) is based on Statius's *Thebaid* and relates the destiny of the children of Oedipus. The *Roman d'Eneas* (*Romance of Aeneas*, around 1160) is an adaptation of Vergil's *Aeneid*. The *Roman de Troie* (*Romance of Troy*) by Benoît de Sainte-Maure (before 1172) is the story of the Trojan War according to the Latin compilations that circulated under the name of Dares Phrygius. Wace's *Roman de Brut* (*Romance of Brut*, 1155), to which I will return shortly, is likewise related to these so-called "romances of antiquity" by its title, its prologue, and its initial subject, the migration of Brutus, the great-grandson of Aeneas, from Latium to Great Britain.

The authors of these romances were of course clerks who were able to read and translate Latin. They claimed, even when it was far from true, to have followed their model with the greatest respect and fidelity. They were proud of the historical and philological competence that enabled them to choose the best source, to translate it exactly, and thus to provide those of their contemporaries who were ignorant of Latin with accurate information about the great events of the past. This is the concept of their task set forth in the long prologue to the *Roman de Troie*. Although it would later become the freest of all genres, romance was thus imprisoned, in its beginnings, within the narrow confines of translation, and its only proclaimed ambition was to tell the historical truth. The genre was called the *roman*, or romance, because it was a *mise en roman*, which is to say, a translation from Latin into the romance language.

The authors of these works did not, however, deny themselves the right to embroider on their models, and not merely by adapting them anachronistically to the civilization of their own time. They reduced the role played by mythology, turned rather towards a "marvelous" based on magic or necromancy, and made multiple additions to their models. But above all, they gave a prominent and altogether new role to love. They amplified the amorous episodes they found in their sources and invented new ones. They described eagerly and at length the birth of love, the confusion of a virgin heart hesitating to acknowledge that it loves, the bashfulness of lovers, their ruses, their evasions, their daring, their betrayals, their secrets, their confessions. The genre's interest in such amorous questions made it particularly receptive to courtliness and courtly love. Even though neither one is clearly recognizable in the romances of antiquity, love was, even at this early stage, the great preoccupation of romance.

In the romances of antiquity, however, this preoccupation was still masked by the declared intention to write history. And not just any history. The romances of antiquity formed a series relating the history of a single family from the time of the Trojan war—and even before, since the history of Thebes, through the intermediary of Jason and the Argonauts, constitutes a sort of Trojan prehistory—and of its foundation of two nations: Aeneas fleeing Troy for Latium and, later, Brutus leaving Latium for Great Britain. The creation of this vast dynastic fresco in a series of literary works was motivated by a political intention. This is clear when one considers that Wace, the author of the *Roman de Brut,* and Benoît de Sainte-Maure, the author of the *Roman de Troie,* both also wrote histories of the ancestors of the king of England, Henry II Plantagenet, going back to the establishment of the Viking Rollo in Normandy— Wace in his *Roman de Rou (Romance of Rou),* Benoît in his *Chronique des ducs de Normandie (Chronicle of the Dukes of Normandy).* This series of works was intended to establish a link between the Anglo-Norman monarchy and the events and the most prestigious heroes of antiquity. If the French monarchs boasted of Charlemagne, the Plantagenets could boast of Aeneas.

But an apparently circumstantial aspect of this enterprise changed the destiny of the romance genre entirely. As long as the romances' action took place in antiquity and their sources were classical, their claim to historical truth could be maintained. When the action moved to the British Isles and the romancers began to use the work of contemporary historians as their sources, when King Arthur succeeded Brutus, the claim to historical truth became untenable.

Wace's *Roman de Brut* is essentially an adaptation of the *Historia regum Britanniae* (*History of the Kings of Britain*) published in 1136 by the Welsh clerk, and later bishop, Geoffrey of Monmouth. Inspired by an ardent "Breton," which is to say Celtic, nationalism, Geoffrey devoted a great deal of his history to King Arthur, who, according to tradition, had fought the Saxon invaders at the beginning of the sixth century, to his father Uther, to the wizard Merlin, their protector, and to all the wonders and prodigies of the magnificent reign Geoffrey attributed to Arthur. Wace improved on the story and was the first to mention the Round Table. But other historians of Henry II's court had their doubts about what Geoffrey had written concerning Arthur and the marvels of Britain. In them they saw only "fables." Everyone was enchanted by them, but no one believed them. No one even pretended to believe them. Wace himself was openly sceptical on the topic of Arthur's reign, even though it was the subject of half of his romance. The Arthurian world, which became the privileged framework for romances in the second half of the twelfth century, made no claim to be true. When it left antiquity and the Mediterranean world, romance renounced historical, referential truth and had to find another kind of truth, a truth of meaning, nourished mainly by a reflection on chivalry and love. From the 1170s on, this search for a new kind of truth would be the work of Chrétien de Troyes, whose great talent established the enduring model of courtly Arthurian romance and its quest for meaning.

Chrétien de Troyes

As is the case with many medieval authors who wrote before the fourteenth century, all we know of Chrétien is what we can deduce from his work and from his successors' allusions to it. We will never know if the Christianus, canon of the abbey of Saint-Loup in Troyes, who is mentioned in a charter of 1173, is the same person as our romancer. He calls himself Chrétien de Troyes in his first romance, *Erec et Enide* (*Erec and Enide*), and simply Chrétien everywhere else. His successors refer to him in both ways. A number of indications suggest he was a clerk, and this is confirmed by Wolfram von Eschenbach who calls him "Von Troys Meister Cristjân" ("Master Christian of Troyes") in *Parzifal*, his adaptation of Chrétien's *Conte du Graal* (*Story of the Grail*).

The only thing known with any certainty about Chrétien is that he was in contact first with the court of Champagne, then with that of Flanders. The *Chevalier de la Charrette* (*Knight of the Cart*) was written in response to a command by the countess Marie de Champagne, to whom the work is dedicated. The *Conte du Graal* is dedicated to Philippe d'Alsace, count of Flanders. Marie de Champagne was the daughter of the king of France, Louis VII the Young, and Eleanor of Aquitaine. As we have already seen, Marie was the patroness of Andreas Capellanus and played an essential role in the diffusion of the courtly spirit and its amorous casuistry in northern France. The exaltation of the adulterous love of Lancelot and Queen Guinevere in the *Chevalier de la Charrette* seems to reflect her conception of love rather than that of the romancer. He himself suggests as much and let someone else finish the romance for him, albeit according to his indications. Chrétien could have met and entered the service of Philippe d'Alsace in 1182 when Philippe, the unofficial regent of the kingdom during Philippe Augustus's minority, came to Troyes to ask, in vain, for the hand of the recently widowed Countess Marie.

At the beginning of *Cligès*, Chrétien names his previous works. In this list are mentioned *Erec et Enide*, several lost translations of Ovid, and a poem on "King Mark and Blond Isolde," also lost. As it has come down to us, his *oeuvre* consists of two love songs and five romances: *Erec et Enide* (around 1170), *Cligès* (around 1176), *Le Chevalier au Lion* (*The Knight with the Lion*) and *Le Chevalier de la Charrette*, probably written simultaneously between 1177 and 1181, and *Le Conte du Graal*, begun between 1182 and 1190 and left unfinished, undoubtedly because of the poet's death. The romance *Guillaume d'Angleterre* (*William of England*), whose author calls himself Chrétien, cannot be attributed to our Chrétien with any certainty.

The five romances have obvious common traits. They are all

Arthurian romances. Love plays an important role in all of them, and in the first four, it plays an essential role. Unlike Wace, Chrétien did not choose history for his subject, generation after generation, reign after reign. The action of each romance is concentrated in time and around the central character. Arthur, moreover, is never the hero of the romances even though the events they relate always take place during his reign. He is the judge and the guarantor of chivalrous and amorous values. The Arthurian world is thus an unchanging given framing the evolution and destiny of the protagonist. In Chrétien's romances, in other words, Arthur's reign is extracted from the chronological succession in which it had previously existed. It floats in the past without attachments. It becomes a mythical time, somewhat analogous to the "once upon a time" of tales. The moorings attaching romance to history were thus definitively broken while, at the same time, the subject of romance was reduced to the adventures and the destiny of a single character, to the crucial moments of a life.

In contrast to Geoffrey of Monmouth and Wace, Chrétien not only made no effort to relate the history of Arthur's reign, he assumed that his audience was already so familiar with the Arthurian world that explanations and background information were superfluous. Each particular narrative is presented as a fragment, a tip, of a vast story whose underlying continuity must be mastered by every reader. No romance relates the whole story of King Arthur, Queen Guinevere, the Round Table, its customs, and its knights, whose names the poet simply enumerates in a knowing way when their presence serves to enhance a ceremony, tournament, or festival. To all this is added a mixture of strangeness and familiarity characterizing the progress of the hero and his adventures. Leaving the castle of King Arthur, entering the nearby forest, the knightly hero immediately enters an unknown, alien, and threatening world where, nonetheless, news travels with astonishing speed and where he never ceases to meet people who already know him, sometimes better than he knows himself, and who show him his destiny in an imperious and fragmentary way. Like the hero, the audience evolves in a world of signs that refer, perpetually, knowingly, and enigmatically, to a meaning that is seemingly self-evident and, because it is self-evident, hidden. The world of these romances is fraught with mysteriously conspicuous—and conspicuously mysterious—meaning.

Chrétien's innovations with respect to Arthurian time and the fragmentation of the romance material thus have very important consequences for the meaning of his romances. Because he no longer claimed to relate a referential truth, Chrétien was obliged to suggest that his works proposed some other type of meaning. He did this especially in their prologues. Unlike his predecessors, he does not claim that his source is true—he says nothing about it, or even underlines its insignificance (as in *Erec et Enide*)—but hints, rather, that he alone is responsible for a meaning revealed above all by the *conjointure*, or organization, he gives to his story. This meaning has the value of a lesson and is not the same as the literal meaning of the story; but neither does it enjoy the autonomous existence of the second, "higher," meaning proposed by an allegorical work. Distinct from the literal meaning, this other meaning is nonetheless immanent in the literal meaning and must remain so. The story is not a pretext for the meaning. The adventures experienced by the hero are simultaneously the cause and the sign of his evolution. The external adventure is simultaneously the source and the image of an internal one. For the meaning is altogether bound up with adventure and love. The solitary figure of the knight errant, almost entirely Chrétien's invention, emblematizes the concerns of his romances: the discovery of one's self, of love, and of the other.

Chrétien stands out as much for his unique tone, style, and type of narration as for the new orientation he gave to romance. The predominant component in his tone is humor, manifesting itself in the distance he puts—not constantly, but lightly, from time to time—between himself and his characters and the situations in which he places them. By means of an aside or a remark, he underlines the contradictions or the mechanical aspect of a behavior or a situation, shows what is unexpected, or too expected, about them, lucidly exposes a character's blindness. This light tone and humor are enhanced by a distinctive style; an easy, rapid, gliding style making good use of the verse. Chrétien was the first to "break" the octosyllabic couplet. Instead of forcing their syntax into the mold of the line or the couplet and being hammered by its rhythm, his sentences are

out of sync with the couplet. They play with the ruptures between the couplet's rhythm and their own. They do not limit
themselves to two lines, but run longer, with new starts and
subordinations. To this broken couplet are added ellipses,
contractions, a brevity of expression that goes well with the sup-
pleness and the naturalness born from breaking the couplet.

Chrétien de Troyes not only marked an important stage in
the development of French literature, he remains one of the
greatest French authors of all time.

The Question of Celtic Sources: The Breton Lay

Chrétien treated his sources with great freedom; but he did not
altogether invent the stories he told. Nor did Geoffrey of Monmouth and Wace. The former, in fact, explicitly declared that
he used Breton sources. The names, the events, the motifs, the
type of marvelous, sometimes even the very stories one finds in
the works of these two authors, of Chrétien, and of his successors, have counterparts and echoes in Celtic—mainly Irish and
Welsh—folklore and texts. One encounters King Arthur and his
companions, or characters who bear the same name as those of
Chrétien and have adventures similar to theirs (Owein, Peredur,
and Gereint who correspond to Yvain, Perceval, and Erec) in
the *Mabinogion*, a collection of Welsh stories in prose including
Breudwyt Rhonabwy (*The Dream of Rhonabwy*) and *Culhwch ac
Olwen* (*Culhwch and Olwen*). But in the state in which they have
come down to us, preserved in thirteenth-century manuscripts,
these texts are later than the French romances and seem to have
been at least partially influenced by them. However, the originality and antiquity of the various Celtic literatures and traditions are so well proven, and the parallels between the Welsh
stories and the French romances so constant and so striking,
that it is impossible not to believe that the latter borrowed from
the former. Despite Edmond Faral's excessive scepticism,[1] and
as other critics like Roger Sherman Loomis and Jean Marx have
maintained,[2] there is no doubt that Geoffrey of Monmouth

---

[1] E. Faral, *La Légende arthurienne*, 3 vols. (Paris: Champion, 1929).

[2] J. Marx, *La Légende arthurienne et le Graal* (Paris: Presses Universitaires
de France, 1952); R. S. Loomis, *Arthurian Tradition and Chrétien de Troyes*
(New York: Columbia Univ. Press, 1949).

borrowed from Celtic sources and that French romancers subsequently did the same, directly or indirectly. This does not at all mean, of course, that it is possible or legitimate to reduce their works to these sources.

In one case at least the French poet explained the work of adaptation she undertook. This poet is Marie de France, undoubtedly a contemporary of Chrétien de Troyes, whose surname indicates simply that, although she lived in Great Britain, she was a native of the Ile-de-France. Her masterwork is a collection of twelve lays, here meaning short stories in verse (the word also refers to a lyrical musical genre). In the general prologue to this collection, Marie declares that she decided to adapt Breton lays into French so that they would not be forgotten; and at the beginning of each lay she is careful to mention its origin and Breton roots, giving its title in the original language, for example, or indicating the precise place to which the legend is attached. For instance:

> Une aventure vus dirai
> Dunt li Bretun firent un lai.
> *Laüstic* ad nun, ceo m'est vis,
> Si l'apelent en leur païs;
> Ceo est «russignol» en franceis
> Et «nihtegale» en dreit engleis.
> En Seint Mallo....
> > (*Laüstic*, 1–7)

(I will tell you of an adventure about which the Bretons made a lay. Its name is *Laüstic*: that's what they call it, I believe, in their country. This means "rossignol" in French and "nightingale" in good English. In Saint-Malo....)

One of Marie's lays is Arthurian (*Lanval*), another is linked to the legend of Tristan (*Chèvrefeuille* [*Honeysuckle*]). About an equal number of anonymous lays survive in addition to Marie's and a comparison of the two groups supports rather than contradicts Marie's declarations. Their motifs and characters are to be found not only in folklore, but specifically, for some of them, in Celtic folklore: supernatural white animals, werewolves, fairy mistresses, water-marked frontiers of the Other World, lovers from other worlds, or from the depths of rivers and lakes, or from the skies. Even the word *lai* is a Celtic word meaning a song, thus justifying the second meaning that it acquired in French.

It is impossible to deny that there are Celtic echoes in French "Breton" literature. And if the authors sometimes claim that these echoes are more numerous in their works than they really are, they only provide further confirmation of the seductiveness of this universe for them and for their readers. But what was the basis of this seductiveness? How ought one to interpret the intensity of the echoes not only of Celtic mythology, but, more broadly, of Indo-European mythology in French romances whose organization and evident interests seem of so different an order? In these works, and especially in the works of Chrétien, it is possible, for example, to discern an attention to calendrical time and its tangle of hagiographical and mythological traditions so precise that it cannot be attributed to chance and its value cannot be measured adequately in terms of the literary composition. The problems and questions posed by the links between this literature and myths or between this literature and what we call folklore are not so much problems and questions of sources as problems and questions of interpretation.

Tristan and Isolde

Why treat the lovers of Cornwall, Tristan and Isolde, separately? Do they not belong to the Breton world and the Breton romances? In French literature, were they not finally integrated into the Arthurian world? Nonetheless, they cannot be reduced to any norm. Their story was known very early and cited everywhere, but only fragments of the first French romances about them have survived. They are both love's model and foils for model lovers. Chrétien was never able to get away from them and never succeeded in conjuring the curse he saw hanging over them. Rarely have literary heroes enjoyed such ambiguous glory.

Even though the evidence is either of uncertain date or difficult to interpret, it seems that the troubadours knew of Tristan and Isolde by the middle of the twelfth century—before Chrétien, before Wace even. For them, Tristan's passion quickly became the standard for, and the measure of, all love, and the play on the words "triste / Tristan" ("sad / Tristan"), ever more frequent in subsequent versions of the story, seems to have been ancient. Other evidence suggests that the story was already in circulation in the first half of the twelfth century. The storyteller Breri, whom Thomas invokes as an authority in his *Roman de Tristan* (*Romance of Tristan*, c. 1172–1175), is certainly the same person as the Bleheris mentioned twenty years later in the *Seconde continuation de Perceval* (*Second Continuation of Perceval*) and the "Bledhericus famosus ille fabulator" ("that famous storyteller Bledhericus") who, according to the description of Wales written by Gerald of Wales around 1180, was active before 1150. He has also been identified, with some likelihood, with the Welsh knight Bledri ap Cadifor, named in documents composed between 1116 and 1135.

In any case, there is no doubt that the legend was known at an early date and was of Celtic origin. *Tóraigheacht Dhiarmada agus Ghráinne* (*The Pursuit of Diarmaid and Gráinne*), an Irish *aithed*, or tale of elopement, going back to at least the ninth century, offers very close parallels to the story of Tristan and Isolde in some of its most precise details as well as in its overall plot. The Welsh Triads, known to us, it is true, only in late manuscripts, mention several times a Drystan or Trystan, son of Tallwch, lover of Essylt, the wife of his uncle King March. Tristan is associated with King Arthur in the Triads and is said to be one of his close advisors.

Despite the precocious popularity of the legend, a sort of curse seems to have struck the first French works devoted to it. Two have been lost altogether (a phenomenon that is rarer than is sometimes believed): the romance of an author called La Chievre and Chrétien's poem on "King Mark and Blond Isolde." The others are fragmentary, either because their authors chose to relate only one particular episode, as in the case of Marie de France's *Chèvrefeuille* and the two versions of the *Folie Tristan* (*Tristan's Madness*), or because they survive in mutilated form, like the romances of Béroul and Thomas. In order to reconstruct the whole story, one must turn to the German romances of Eilhart von Oberge and Gottfried von Strassburg, inspired by the French works, and the Norse *Tristrams saga ok Isöndar* (*The Saga of Tristam and Isolde*). This is an intriguing state of affairs, the effect, it has been suggested, of a kind of censorship. And it is true that the legend troubled its medieval French audiences as much as it fascinated them. Faithful to courtly orthodoxy, the poets—Chrétien among them in one of his two surviving songs—proclaimed the superiority of their love to Tristan's, for they had chosen freely to love, while he had been constrained to do so by the power of the potion. In *Cligès*, Chrétien refers openly to the situation of Tristan and Isolde and tries—without any real success—to make it more morally acceptable by enabling his heroine to avoid having to sleep with her husband as well as her lover. But these reservations did not diminish the legend's immense success, nor do they in any way explain the fragmentary character of the first French poems inspired by it. This fragmentary character is, rather, the consequence of a popularity that enabled and encouraged authors to narrate an episode or portion of the story without retelling or recopying the whole history from beginning to end.

Béroul's romance (c. 1190?), whose middle section has been preserved, relates the so-called "common" version of *Tristan et Iseut* (*Tristan and Isolde*), while Thomas's romance, of which we possess several separate fragments and the end, relates the so-called "courtly" version. One of the differences between the two is that the effect of the potion lasts for only a limited time in Béroul's version, but lasts for life in Thomas's, making it a symbol of love. But the main difference between the two versions is their style. Rougher, Béroul writes with an effective simplicity that makes no effort to analyze the protagonists' feelings and, indeed, his romance draws its strength from this conciseness. Thomas, on the other hand, combines a virtuoso— and sometimes slightly self-satisfied—rhetoric with a keen and intense perception of the lovers' passion.

The "Breton" Romance and the Heritage of Chrétien

The profound influence Chrétien's romances exercised on subsequent medieval French literature manifested itself in several ways. His romances were imitated. They supplied the subject of the first prose romances. They produced an immediate reaction among the rivals of the master from Champagne, who took great pains to affirm their own originality but were constrained to define themselves in relation to him.

Chrétien's romances were imitated and the Arthurian verse

romance, henceforward a distinct literary genre, was immensely
successful through the second half of the thirteenth century
when its popularity was definitively overtaken by that of the
prose romance. It retained the characteristics Chrétien had
given it. Romance authors liked to trace the amorous and
chivalric apprenticeship of a young hero through a series of
adventures that are deliberately marvelous and very often take
the form of a quest. When the hero is as well-established a
knight and lover as Arthur's nephew Gawain, the romancers are
content simply to recount his exploits. In this family of romances one finds works like Renaut de Beaujeu's *Le Bel Inconnu* (*The
Handsome Stranger*), Paien de Mézières's *La Mule sans frein* (*The
Mule without a Bit*), *Le Chevalier à l'épée* (*The Knight with the
Sword*), Raoul de Houdenc's *Meraugis de Portlesguez* (*Meraugis
of Portlesguez*), *La Vengeance Raguidel* (*The Avenging of Raguidel*;
this also has been attributed to Raoul), *Humbaut*, *L'Atre péril-
leux* (*The Perilous Hearth*), Robert de Blois's *Beaudous*, *Fergus*,
Yder, *Durmart le Gallois* (*Durmart the Welshman*), *Le Chevalier
aux deux épées* (*The Knight with Two Swords*), *Les Merveilles de
Rigomer* (*The Wonders of Rigomer*), the interminable *Claris et
Laris* (*Claris and Laris*), *Floriant et Florete* (*Floriant and Florete*),
Escanor, *Gliglois*, and, in the language of *oc*, *Jaufré*. Beate
Schmolke-Hasselmann has argued plausibly that the verse
romance, already out of fashion on the continent by the second
half of the thirteenth century, survived in the culturally conser-
vative milieu of the Anglo-Norman court.[1] It was for this court
that Froissart composed the first version of his *Méliador*, the last
link in this tradition, at the end of the fourteenth century, when
no one had written an Arthurian verse romance for over a
hundred years.

But Chrétien's influence was most fertile in the area of a
very particular subject and theme: the Grail. As was mentioned
earlier, his last romance, *Le Conte du Graal*, remained unfinished. At the Grail castle, Perceval fails to ask the question that
would heal his cousin, the Fisher King; he then wanders for five
years, far from God and men, before confessing to his uncle,

[1] B. Schmolke-Hasselmann, *Der arthurische Versroman von Chrestien bis
Froissart: Zur Geschichte einer Gattung* (Tübingen: M. Niemayer, 1980).

the hermit. The reader senses that he is now ready to succeed where he failed the first time, but the romance has nothing more to say about him; it goes on to relate the adventures of Gawain and breaks off in the middle of one of them. An admirable romance, a fascinating subject: how could one bear not knowing the ending? So continuations were added to the *Conte du Graal*. Far from bringing the romance to an end, the first continuation, written in the first years of the thirteenth century, does not even get around to Perceval. It merely continues, and not without talent, to relate the adventures of Gawain. The second, attributed to Wauchier de Denain but in reality anonymous, does indeed continue the adventures of Perceval, but it, too, is unfinished. Between 1233 and 1237, a third continuation by a certain Manessier finally brings the story to an end: Perceval succeeds his cousin the Fisher King as lord of the Grail castle. Between 1225 and 1230, a poet named Gerbert, perhaps the Gerbert of Montreuil who wrote the *Roman de la Violette* (*Romance of the Violet*), composed another continuation, independent of the other three, which, despite its 17,000 lines, does not altogether bring to a close the ultimate adventure of the Grail. Manessier and Gerbert accent the religious aspect of the story, already discreetly present in Chrétien's romance. But this tendency to Christianize the Grail is far more evident in the earlier work of Robert de Boron.

A knight from the Franche-Comté, Robert de Boron composed a verse romance, the *Roman de l'estoire du Graal* or *Joseph d'Arimathie* (*Romance of the Story of the Grail* or *Joseph of Arimathea*), written no later than 1215. In this poem, the Grail becomes a Christian relic, the cup used at the Last Supper, in which Joseph of Arimathea subsequently caught Christ's blood as he hung on the cross. Later, Robert de Boron wrote a *Merlin*, of which only the first 500 lines survive, but it is also known to us through a prose adaptation. He was probably also the author of a *Perceval*, of which, according to some scholars, the *Didot-Perceval* is the prose adaptation. These three works formed a first Grail cycle preceding the prose *Lancelot-Grail* cycle. Robert de Boron's work was an important turning point in the treatment of the Grail material for two reasons. First, he imposed— definitively—a religious and mystic interpretation on the Grail. Second, the destiny of these works, written in verse but quickly

adapted into prose, is intimately bound up with the appearance
of the first prose romances, which were Grail romances based in
many ways on the romances of Chrétien de Troyes, as we will
see in the following chapter.

Both the traditional verse romances and the new prose
romances of the thirteenth century thus owe a great deal, in
different ways, to the work of Chrétien.

The Many Paths of Adventure

While Chrétien was still alive, his colleague and rival Gautier
d'Arras reproached both him, without naming him, and other
amateurs of the Breton marvelous with telling incredible stories
that made those who heard them think they were dreaming
rather than awake. This was the beginning of a reaction against
Chrétien's influence, a reaction often, but incorrectly, termed
"realist." The romancers who reacted against Chrétien's influence did not in any way contest his essential contribution. Like
him, they implicitly admitted the fictive nature of romance and
made no claim whatsoever to historical or referential truth.
Their concept of verisimilitude was simply a little different from
his and they preferred to avoid the mythical mists of the Arthurian world. The action of *Ille et Galeron* (*Ille and Galeron*),
Gautier's first romance, moves from Brittany to Rome; his
second romance, *Eracle*, is something between a romance of
antiquity and a saint's life, since the model for his hero is the
Byzantine emperor Heraklios and the romance's second part is
based on the legend of the discovery of the Holy Cross. Jean
Renart, who, like Gautier, delivers a polemical elegy of verisimilitude in his first romance, *L'Escoufle* (*The Kite*, around 1200),
is otherwise entirely unlike him. A brilliant stylist, a malicious
and subtle mind, able to disconcert without seeming to and to
overturn the commonplaces he feigned to use, he could do a
great deal with nothing and took pleasure in generic settings,
depicting with grace and humor scenes that only appear to be
quotidian. In his *Roman de la Rose ou de Guillaume de Dole*
(*Romance of the Rose or of Guillaume of Dole*, around 1212 or
1228, according to different scholars), he was the first to insert
lyric pieces in a romance, a technique that subsequently enjoyed
great success throughout the rest of the Middle Ages and one
whose interest and function he explains with evident pride in

the prologue. He was quickly imitated, in this and other ways, by Gerbert de Montreuil in his *Roman de la Violette ou de Gérard de Nevers* (*Romance of the Violet or of Gerard of Nevers*), while at the end of the century, Jakemes's *Roman du Châtelain de Coucy et de la Dame de Fayel* (*Romance of the Chatelain of Coucy and the Lady of Fayel*) cites poems by the twelfth-century trouvère known as the Châtelain de Coucy, who is also the hero of the romance.

Jean Renart is likewise the author of a sort of courtly short story, the delightful *Lai de l'ombre* (*Lay of the Shadow*). This poem is not altogether unique. Certain other poems, like *La châtelaine de Vergi* (*The Chatelaine of Vergi*), *Le vair palefroi* (*The Dappled Palfrey*) of Huon le Roi, and, later, the *Dit du prunier* (*Poem of the Plum Tree*), use the pretext of a very simple intrigue to offer a reflection—or a shadow—of courtly life, of a refinement of manners and feelings they do not feel obliged to transport to the distant Breton universe and dress up in Arthurian accessories. These tales reveal that the elegance one finds in the works of Chrétien also inhabits the contemporary world.

But there is a host of other romances that, without giving any thought to verisimilitude or seeking the bareness of an elegant brevity, simply give themselves up to a passion for adventures in other frameworks and according to other conventions than those of the Arthurian world, like *Ipomedon* and *Protheselaus* by the Norman clerk Hue de Rothelande, who was roughly a contemporary of Chrétien and wrote with a ready pen and a somewhat cynical smuttiness. Or all the romances whose action takes place in the Mediterranean basin, either because they remain faithful to antiquity—for their setting if not for their sources—like *Athis et Prophilias* (*Athis and Prophilias*) and *Florimont*, or because they prolong the Alexandrian tradition of stories of separated lovers who travel the world over in search of one another, like *Floire et Blancheflor* (*Floire and Blancheflor*) or, to some degree, *Partonopeus de Blois* (*Partonopeus of Blois*), in which the fairy mistress plays an interesting role. In the thirteenth century, these diverse romances of adventure, nourished with various leftovers, with borrowings from folklore and myth, with diverse phantasms—like the incest in Philippe de Remi's *La Manekine* (*The Manikin*), in Jehan Maillart's *Roman du comte d'Anjou* (*Romance of the Count of Anjou*), in the *Roman de la*

Belle Hélène de Constantinople (*Romance of Beautiful Helen of Constantinople*), in the updated version of the old *Roman d'Apollonius de Tyr* (*Romance of Apollonius of Tyr*)—these romances are as numerous as the Arthurian verse romances. Adapted into prose, many of them—some of those cited above, but also *Blancandin*, Adenet le Roi's *Cléomadès*, and many others— enjoyed a certain success right through to the end of the Middle Ages ... at which point we will return to them.

PART THREE
THE ESTABLISHMENT OF A LITERATURE

The fertile and original development of French literature that began in the twelfth century does not seem to have continued with the same vigor after the first third of the thirteenth century. The principal literary forms were in place by then and, from our perspective, they seem to have been simply maintained, and sometimes exhausted, rather than renewed. Although it is not entirely false, this impression should not prevent us from grasping the importance of the thirteenth century.

The thirteenth century was critical, assimilating and organizing the achievements and acquisitions of the preceding century in all domains of intellectual life. It was the age of encyclopedias—*specula*, or "mirrors," as they were then called—and of *summae*, or "compendiums." The *Summa theologica* of Saint Thomas Aquinas, for example, is a synthesis of a body of theological reflection that had been developing with an extreme, but sometimes disorganized and, in the eyes of the Church, even dangerous, vigor since the end of the eleventh century. The triple "mirror"—the *Speculum naturale, doctrinale, historiale* (*The Natural, Doctrinal, and Historical Mirror*)—of Vincent of Beauvais, another Dominican, is a monument of erudition which sought to bring together all the knowledge of its time. Universities appeared during this period and, developing rapidly, undertook to organize and disseminate this knowledge. In the domain of literature there was also an effort toward organization and reflection, and French literature began timidly to admit of intellectual speculation.

Because of the conditions underlying its diffusion and practice, literature did not really merit its name, from the word *letters*, until the thirteenth century. It was then that the circulation of texts was truly developed and organized. Twelfth-century French literary manuscripts are rare and the works of that period are known to us principally through manuscripts copied in the thirteenth century, when French literature truly entered the written world. The development of prose, the great innovation of this century, is undoubtedly related to this movement. At the same time, the text was ever more deliberately defined as the reflection of a consciousness, and the signs permitting the identification of a literary "I" multiplied. As a result, literary genres were distributed and interpreted in new ways.

6   *The Birth of Prose: Romance and Chronicle*

Up until the end of the twelfth century, French literature was written entirely in verse; literary prose did not exist. The only texts in vernacular prose, and there were not many of them, were of a utilitarian—juridical or edifying—nature, charters or translations of the Scripture or sermons. This situation is characteristic of all young literatures: everywhere verse appears before prose. It is surprising only that this occurs even when people know and use prose in another language. Latin prose, for instance, appeared after Latin poetry, even though the Romans knew Greek prose—whose own appearance dated to three centuries after that of Greek poetry. Similarly, the fact that the Middle Ages knew and wrote Latin prose from the very beginning did nothing to prevent the usual delay in the development of French prose. When literary French prose did appear, it took two forms, the romance and the chronicle. Its appearance thus partially reestablished, although, at least in the beginning, in an altogether formal way, the link between history and stories that had been broken by Chrétien-like romances. In general, prose always claimed to be true.

The First Prose Romances

A trilogy on the Grail story was written in prose around 1220. As we saw in the preceding chapter, it was made up in part, or perhaps entirely, of the prose adaptations of the romances of Robert de Boron. It consisted of the *Roman de l'estoire dou Graal* (*Romance of the Story of the Grail*), the *Merlin*, and the prose *Perceval*, also called the *Didot-Perceval* or the *Perceval de Modène* (*Perceval of Modena*) after the two manuscripts containing it. These three romances recount the history of the Grail and of the family into whose keeping it was given from Christ's Passion up to the time of Perceval's adventures and the collapse of the

Arthurian world. Between 1225 and 1230 another, far greater, prose Grail cycle appeared, the enormous collection known as the *Lancelot-Grail*, or Vulgate, cycle. Its first innovation, evident in its name, was to shift its focus from Perceval to Lancelot and his family, and thus to attach itself to Chrétien's *Chevalier de la charrette* (*Knight of the Cart*), to the Lancelot who is willing to dishonor himself in the eyes of the world for love of Guinevere, as well as to Chrétien's *Conte du Graal* (*Story of the Grail*). The kernel of the cycle, the so-called *Lancelot propre* (*Lancelot Proper*), accounts for about two-thirds of the whole collection. It is dedicated entirely to the birth of Lancelot, his childhood, his adventures, and the love that makes him the best knight in the world. But in the *Queste del saint Graal* (*Quest for the Holy Grail*), the next work in the series, Lancelot's adulterous love for the queen excludes him from the mysteries of the Grail, accessible only to his son, Galaad, his cousin Bohort, and Perceval. This love is also the indirect cause of the final catastrophe that brings about the dissolution of the Arthurian world in the *Mort le roi Artu* or *Mort Artu* (*Death of King Arthur* or *Death of Arthur*), the last work in the cycle. Two other works adapted from Robert de Boron's trilogy, the *Histoire du Graal* (*Story of the Grail*) and *Merlin*, were attached to the beginning of the cycle at a later date. The cycle's "double spirit"—amorous and courtly in the *Lancelot*, then ascetic and mystical in the *Queste*—is surprising. The *Mort Artu*, moreover, has yet another tonality: gloomy, pessimistic, tormented by a fatalism from which God seems absent. Was the cycle the work of several authors? Undoubtedly, but on the other hand, the composition of the whole collection is extraordinarily rigorous. There are very few contradictions, with agreement even between tiny details separated by hundreds, or thousands, of pages. It is reasonable to suppose, as Jean Frappier suggested, that an "architect" planned the whole cycle which was then realized by several writers, but this does little more than reformulate the problem. In truth, the cycle's "double spirit," its vertiginous and mysterious mixture of diversity and unity founded on a sort of dialectic between worldly perfection and ascetic and mystical perfection, is not necessarily the sign of a contradiction or of two antagonistic ideologies.

Finally, a rather strange romance, the *Haut livre du Graal*

(*High Book of the Grail*) or *Perlesvaus*, dated by some scholars to the first years of the thirteenth century, while others suggest that it was written after the *Lancelot-Grail* cycle, presents itself as a sort of prose continuation of the *Conte du Graal*. It takes certain liberties with the information furnished by Chrétien, however, and relates the successive quests of Gawain, Lancelot, and Perlesvaus (Perceval), who, after the death of the Fisher King, retakes the Grail castle from a usurper.

The first prose romances in French, then, were Grail romances. This was probably not, or not only, due to chance. The prosaic character of these works, which might seem accidental to us, was perfectly clear to contemporaries. The translator of the *Philippide*, a Latin epic glorifying the French king Philip Augustus, declares in a verse prologue that he will write in prose, taking as his model "the book of Lancelot, in which there is not a single word of verse." A century later, Guilhem Molinier, states that he will exclude prose works from his *Leys d'Amors* (*Lay of Love*), a Provençal treatise on grammar and poetics, and names "the Romance of the Holy Grail" as an example and emblem of the kinds of works excluded from his study.

Why this association between prose and the Grail? Probably because of the association between prose and religious literature. The prose romances appeared at the moment when Grail literature took on a mystical coloring, when worldly glory and courtly love ceased to be exalted and began to be stigmatized as sinful, when Galaad became the new knightly Christ who had come to complete the work of redemption. The only models of French prose available to the romancers were religious texts: sermons, edifying treatises, saints' lives translated from Latin. In Latin, moreover, the sacred was always expressed in prose. Prose was the language of exegesis and preaching. It was the language of the Bible, the language not only of the New Testament and the historical books of the Old, but of all Holy Scripture since Isidore of Seville's extension of the term *prosa* to everything not composed according to classical Latin metrics. This meant that even the Latin translations of the Bible's poetic texts, the Psalms or the Song of Solomon, could be grouped in the category of prose. Prose, in sum, was the language of God. If one thinks of it, as did Isidore, as a direct mode of expression, writing *in a straight line*, as opposed to the slitherings of the poetic line subject to metric constraint, one implicitly grants that it is more nearly adequate to the idea to be expressed, which is not hidden or falsified by detours and ornaments. In the Platonic climate of medieval Christianity, this trait made prose preferable to verse. It could hardly be imagined that God's word should bend to the frivolous laws of poetry, an idea that shows, moreover, how far medieval literature was from being primitive: poetry was not the language of the sacred in the medieval aesthetic system. Prose was thus more than the language of religious literature, it was the language of the Bible; and more than that, it was the language of God. A book that revealed God's plan had to be in prose. The Grail romances had to be in prose because they traced the family history of the guardians of the mystical vase, from Joseph of Arimathea to Galaad or Perceval; because this history was bound up, supposedly, with the salvation of all humanity and was endowed with an eschatological meaning linked to the mystery of redemption. They had to be in prose, finally, because the history they related developed around the ultimate words of divine revelation, a kernel simultaneously empty and full, always concealed and always at work. The narrator's prose held the place, and stood as a sign, of God's prose, as did, for example, the prose of the priest Blaise, the confessor of Merlin's mother and the supposed recorder of his history.

Finally, and more precisely, the stylistic details of these romances were frequently inspired by Holy Scripture or by homiletic literature, thus revealing their true models. The prose adaptations of Robert de Boron's works, for example, sometimes depart from the original verse text in order to translate directly the scriptural passage providing the general inspiration for that text. And the *Queste del saint Graal* imitates the methods and discourse of exegesis and preaching in giving a role to allegory in the interpretation of the world and of divine signs.

Prose was thus linked to truth. It was commonplace among prose authors in the Middle Ages to declare that prose was truer than verse and that, unlike verse, it made no sacrifice to ornament. In the Grail romances, prose served to express a truth of both a spiritual and a historical order. For in fixing the genealogy of the Grail's guardians, these romances bound themselves back into the history from which the Arthurian world had been abstracted by Chrétien. One should thus not be surprised to see that prose was taken up simultaneously by the romancers and, as we will soon see, by the chroniclers writing history in French.

Of course the link between prose and spiritual preoccupations disappeared as soon as prose began to be used more widely. This happened very quickly since its dissemination was favored by the spread of writing, by its growing familiarity to romance audiences, and by the development of individual reading. As I have already noted, the atmosphere of the last part of the *Lancelot-Grail* cycle, the *Mort le roi Artu,* is strangely secular. The same observation could be made about the immense prose *Tristan* written shortly before the middle of the century, whose success is attested by its survival in eighty-some manuscripts. This romance marks the definitive mixture of the legends of Tristan and Arthur. Because of the high number of variant readings from one manuscript version to another—variants sometimes extending to whole episodes—this romance also marks the beginning of a sort of textual *mouvance,* an ongoing textual evolution, which the Breton prose romances experienced at the end of the Middle Ages. Already the author of *Guiron le Courtois* (*Courtly Guiron*), written very shortly after the prose *Tristan,* tried to fit his work into the *Lancelot-Grail* cycle. When it comes to later works, the modern reader is lost in a labyrinth of copies and compilations. In putting together his *Roman de Roi Artus* (*Romance of King Arthur*) or *Compilation,* Rusticiano da Pisa—who likewise recorded Marco Polo's account of his adventures in the *Livre des merveilles* (*Book of Wonders*)—borrowed from both the prose *Tristan* and *Guiron le Courtois.* One can also follow across manuscripts, in silhouette as it were, the traces of a "Pseudo-Robert de Boron cycle" not preserved whole in any manuscript. More than verse, prose invited revision "in reading, in writing." From copy to copy, successive generations of readers reshaped it according to their tastes.

Chronicles: From Latin to French, from Verse to Prose

History was normally written in Latin throughout most of the Middle Ages. The moment (relatively late) that best symbolizes the birth of French historiography is undoubtedly that when the ongoing history of the kings of France kept at Saint-Denis (the *Grandes chroniques de France* [*Great Chronicles of France*]) was first translated into French (1274–1350), then continued directly in that language. But, as we have seen, the writing of history and the writing of romance overlapped in a complex system from the moment the romance genre emerged. Soon thereafter, as romances turned increasingly towards fiction, French chronicles appeared in which may be seen, albeit in a somewhat artificial fashion, the beginnings of historiography in the French language.

The attention paid to history and the desire to write history were significant aspects of the intellectual renewal of the Carolingian period. They were motivated by concerns that were simultaneously immediate and fundamental, political and speculative. Charlemagne had the annals of his reign written for his greater glory. At the same time, reflection on the ways of God and the history of salvation brought about an effort to discover and write the history of all humanity. Following a model going back to the patristic period, repeated attempts were made to establish universal chronologies synthesizing Biblical history and the history of pagan antiquity. Annals, chronicles, and history were considered distinct genres involving different degrees of distance from the events and different degrees of intellectual and literary elaboration; annals were the closest to events and involved the least elaboration, history was the furthest and involved the most. The Carolingian historian was a creature of the study, gathering—sometimes buying, selling, or forging—documents, choosing a form of writing, trying to imitate classical models, considering the ways of God and the actions of men. This type of history endured throughout the Middle Ages, although it was inflected by the appearance of a national history whose preoccupations pushed aside those of universal history. It was the desire to write this national history, the effort to bring to light "national" origins (even though the word is still inappropriate at this date) that underlay the composition of the first French romances. The establishment of a continuity between the Trojans and the Plantagenets was a response to the legend of the Trojan origins of the Franks (descendants of Francus), which had generally been accepted since Fredegarius (c. 660) and was a source of great pride for the kings of France.

In the twelfth century, however, more recent history began to be written in French in the new, vernacular poetic forms. The *chanson de geste* was chosen by Jordan Fantosme, even though his versification is rather peculiar, for his history of the campaign of Henry II Plantagenet against the Scots in 1173. It was also chosen for the crusade cycle and, at the beginning of the thirteenth century, for the *Chanson de la croisade albigeoise* (*Song of the Albigensian Crusade*) in the language of *oc*, which declares that it was modeled on the *Chanson d'Antioche* (*Song of Antioch*). The romance form was chosen by Ambroise de Normandie, a jongleur in the service of Richard the Lionhearted, for his account of the Third Crusade, the *Histoire de la guerre sainte* (*History of the Holy War*), written before 1195. Rhymed chronicles relating particular events or celebrating great figures were written throughout the Middle Ages. More ambitious than most—ambitious as only the solitary work of an amateur can be—Philippe Mousket's rhymed chronicle begins with the Trojan War and ends in 1243, drawing abundantly on epic and romance sources.

Prose, however, was the medium of Latin historiography and became the medium of French historiography at the beginning of the thirteenth century, at the same time as the Grail story inaugurated the prose romance. The writers who are usually termed the first French chroniclers were not professional writers and were in reality memorialists. They recounted events they had not only witnessed, but in which they had been involved as participants, and sometimes as important participants. They were driven to write, or dictate, the narrative of these events by the strong impressions they had retained or, more often, for personal reasons linked to the role they had played in them. This was already the case, at the beginning of the twelfth century, for the work known as the *Histoire anonyme de la première croisade* (*Anonymous History of the First Crusade*), written in Latin, to be sure, by the clerk who recorded it, but certainly dictated by a knight, a crusader, who knew only French. A century later, the works of his successors were preserved in French prose. Perhaps they were written in prose rather than in verse because their authors were amateurs; but fifty years earlier no one would have had the idea to write in French prose.

Moreover, the chroniclers' recourse to this new form eventually had a profound effect on the development of both French prose and the romance genre.

The first of these chroniclers were the historians of the Fourth Crusade, Robert de Clari, a modest participant but no dupe, and Geoffroy de Villehardouin, who, despite an affected impartiality and laconic coldness, was eager to justify the political and military decisions for which he was partly responsible. Philippe de Novare, a third important chronicler, wrote a bit later. He, too, was anxious to justify his choices in the political affairs of Cyprus, but his temperament was rather different and his work, now partially lost, was as he himself tells us, a sort of autobiographical construction. At the beginning of the fourteenth century—but he lived to be so old and wrote so late!— Jean de Joinville likewise transformed into an autobiography what was supposed to be a collection of memoirs destined to justify the canonization of Saint Louis. The attention the author pays to himself, his self-representation, grows steadily from the first to the fourth of these "chroniclers," and such authors moved the genre that they made illustrious further and further from the writing of history.

Despite the existence of certain works like the compilation known under the name of the *Histoire ancienne jusqu'à César (Ancient History up until Caesar*, shortly before 1230), based on the Bible, the work of Flavius Josephus, that of Orosius, and the romances of antiquity (the *Roman de Thèbes* [*Romance of Thebes*] is used systematically), the writing of history in French prose did not truly appear and develop in forms other than memoirs until the middle of the fourteenth century. It later flourished and became strong enough to stifle the romance genre to a certain degree, even though the first chronicles and the Grail romances had shared hardly any common points. Everywhere it appeared, and as soon as it appeared, however, prose began to manifest its uniform claim to tell the truth.

7   *Drama and Laughter*

The Dramatic Expression of Literature

In Chapter Two, in the course of a discussion of the oldest French texts, I mentioned the passages in French that were inserted in certain liturgical plays. Theater, however, was not among the forms in which the young French literature first manifested its creativity and independence. It is true that there is little theater in French until the end of the thirteenth century—but this statement is also inadequate and anachronistic insofar as it is founded on modern literary divisions and practices. Medieval French literature was almost exclusively sung or recited. It existed only in performance. It all required staging and dramatic expression. What we call theater was only a special aspect of a general situation. Only a few French plays survive from the twelfth and thirteenth centuries, but all French literature at this time was more or less theatrical. To a certain degree, jongleurs were the heirs of the Latin mimes, as Edmond Faral has shown.[1] Their renderings were indeed very often *dramatized*, and the abundance of dialogues in medieval French literature suggests the effects they were able to produce by imitating the voice of one interlocutor, then the other. An unclassifiable work like the charming *chantefable* (or "song-fable"; the word is not attested elsewhere and seems to have been invented by the author to describe this work) *Aucassin et Nicolette* (*Aucassin and Nicolette*, thirteenth century) appears to have been composed with a "one-man show" of this type in mind. Using multiple dialogues, alternating sections in verse with sections in prose—the former sung and the latter recited, as the manuscript rubrics at the beginning of each section indicate—this good-natured work tells an idyllic little story and

---

[1] E. Faral, *Les Jongleurs en France au Moyen Age* (Paris: Champion, 1910).

rapidly and humorously parades the conventions of the different literary genres. In an altogether different register, Rutebeuf's *Dit de l'herberie* (*Poem of the Herbalist*) is a parody of a charlatan's spiel intended to showcase the talent of the performer, who delivers it second-hand without letting his presence be forgotten.

In the thirteenth century, French literature on the whole evolved in a way that accentuated this general dramatic tendency while modifying its traits and implications. Poetry turned to a deliberate caricaturing of the poetic self, and the laughter it sought to provoke also appeared, under conditions that still need to be elucidated, at the heart of the new dramatic forms. This is why I will discuss together in this chapter first the birth and development of theater—which should be treated separately anyway for the sake of a clear exposition—second, the representation of the poetic self to which poetry increasingly devoted itself, and third, this period's particular forms of literary comedy.

Theater

Because I have not yet discussed theater, let me go back briefly to its first manifestations. No mutation, no rupture separated French theater from medieval Latin religious theater at its beginnings; nothing truly broke the essential continuity between the two. It is as though the proportions of Latin and French in liturgical drama merely changed little by little until the latter eventually took over from the former. The first play entirely in French, the *Jeu d'Adam* (*Play of Adam*), dates to the middle of the twelfth century and is in fact a liturgical drama portraying the creation of humankind and the original sin. Its dependence on Latin and its liturgical role are still very evident. In the manuscript, its title—*Ordo representacionis Ade* (*Plan for the Representation of Adam*)—and its stage directions are in Latin. The text incorporates a reading and seven responses borrowed from the service of Septuagesima Sunday which, sung by the choir, scan the *Jeu* and make it into a sort of gloss on the service. The manuscript contains only the first words of the reading with which the play begins, "In principio creavit Deus celum et terram" ("In the beginning God created the heaven and the earth"), but in conformity with the liturgy, this reading certainly included the entire first chapter of Genesis. The spectators thus first heard in Latin the prologue to the events that they then saw performed in French. Like so many scenes, these events are framed by the responses, each of which thus seems to be a sort of preliminary summary of the dramatic development that follows and illustrates it and whose orthodoxy it guarantees in advance. The dramatic French poem enjoyed a certain liberty, but this could be exercised only in the shadow of the sacred text. The *Jeu* could only amplify and orchestrate—with, it is true, a vigorous density—the few scriptural verses that formed its subject and from which a respect for Holy Scripture would not permit it to stray.

Written fifty years later, the *Jeu de saint Nicolas* (*Play of Saint Nicholas*) by the great trouvère from Arras, Jean Bodel, was still a religious play whose spiritual depth is greater than one might at first think, but it broke all ties with the liturgy—even if it was first performed on the eve of Saint Nicholas's day, probably 5 December 1200—and with Latin, even though many liturgical dramas in that language had presented Saint Nicholas's miracles. Not a single word of Latin remains in the play. Even the prologue, which may not be authentic, and the text's only stage direction are in French. But the play's principal innovation lies elsewhere, in its representation of daily life in Arras, depicted with precision and verve, albeit at the cost of all verisimilitude since the action is situated among the infidels of the "kingdom of Africa." The story of the robbers who covet the king of Africa's treasure that has been placed under the saint's protection is in effect a pretext for long tavern scenes complete with drinking bouts and gambling. Wine from the town of Auxerre in Burgundy is sold and people count in French *deniers* and *mailles* (small coins): Africa is very far away. Was this a mere detail? An accidental circumstance? Perhaps. But from this time on, the few surviving Arras plays, scattered throughout the thirteenth century, turned progressively towards secular subjects and almost systematically incorporated tavern scenes.

Courtois d'Arras (*Courtois of Arras*), for example. Is it a play? It is not absolutely certain if one uses the word in its modern sense, but the poem was written entirely in dialogue and clearly lends itself to performance, whether the dialogue was distributed among several actors or pronounced by a single jongleur

who played all the roles one after another. It is an adaptation of
the parable of the Prodigal Son (Luke 15:11–32). And while
this is still a religious subject, the Gospel sentence most capti-
vating to the author, which he developed most abundantly and
with the greatest enthusiasm, is the one relating that the prodigal son spent his inheritance in debauchery. This is the pretext
for a long and picturesque tavern scene in which one sees the
unhappy young man ruin himself with the help of the innkeeper
and two "hostesses." This episode alone accounts for over half
the text (428 of the poem's 664 lines).

Apart from a short farce entitled *Du Garçon et de l'aveugle*
(*The Boy and the Blind Man*) dating to the middle of the thir-
teenth century, the first examples of a truly secular theater date
to around 1280 and are the work of another poet from Arras,
Adam de la Halle, who was mentioned earlier as a lyric poet.
One of his two plays, the *Jeu de Robin et de Marion* (*The Play of
Robin and Marion*), is more or less the dramatic presentation of
a pastourelle with variations on the different situations presented in these songs. But the other, the *Jeu de la feuillée* (*Play of the
Bower*), is of an altogether different nature. The play's characters are, on the one hand, Adam de la Halle himself, his father,
his friends, his neighbors, all very real individuals; and, on the
other hand, representatives of the crowd on the streets of Arras:
bewildered rustics, suspect friars, shrews with a taste for trifles
or sorcery. At the beginning of the play, Adam, decked out in
clerical finery, believing he is seeing them for the last time, takes
his leave of them, fully determined to continue his studies in
Paris. In the end, however, he remains a prisoner of this nar-
row-minded, grotesque, insignificantly enchanted world—a fairy
scene takes place in the middle of the play—and of a disap-
pointing marriage, and goes off to finish the night in a tavern
with the others.

The tavern is the downfall of the robbers of the *Jeu de saint
Nicolas*, of Courtois, and of Adam, but it is a kind of downfall
that lends itself to laughter—a laughter whose object, in the *Jeu
de la feuillée*, is as much the poet himself as the other characters.
Adam, the principal character of the *feuillée*, is likewise the
principal character of a poem on an analogous theme, the
Congés (*Farewells*). And around the same time, Rutebeuf described in several poems the decadence and the misery to which

tavern life had led him, while in others he expressed his devotion and repentance without any irony in terms very close to those he placed in the mouth of the clerk Théophile in the *Miracle* he devoted to him. If we remember that medieval theater is only artificially distinguished by our anachronistic eye from the dramatic expression coloring the whole of medieval literature, we can perceive the relation between theater and the evolution of poetry in the thirteenth century, an evolution defined above as a caricaturing of the subject, simultaneously self-satisfied and self-critical.

The *Dit*: A Birth of Poetry

The *grand chant courtois* (great courtly song) of the trouvères survived until the end of the thirteenth century. Adam de la Halle himself, an author of varied talents, was one of its last practitioners. But from this time on, poetry moved in other, non-lyric directions. A recited poetry developed, whose origin and conventions had nothing to do with courtly lyricism. It was this kind of poetry that, in large part, gave birth to what we today call "personal poetry" or even "lyric poetry," in the common use of this expression that no longer refers to song. It is likewise this recited poetry—the *dit* (spoken) as opposed to the sung—that provided the framework for the dramatization of the self.

The first inspiration of this poetry was simultaneously moral, religious, and satirical. From the middle of the twelfth century, it developed in the form of verse "sermons," reviews of social categories or "estates of the world" denouncing the vices of each; but it tended, around 1200, to take root in the poet's particular experience and point of view. Around 1190, such verse sermons appeared at the beginning and the end of Hélinand de Froidmont's *Vers de la Mort* (*Verses on Death*), whose success and influence were considerable and whose stanzaic form was very often imitated. In 1202, this same verse form nourished and structured in an infinitely more radical and dramatic fashion the *Congés* (*Farewells*) of Jean Bodel, the author of the *Jeu de saint Nicolas*, who had become a leper; and, seventy years later those of another poet from Arras who had likewise become a leper, Baude Fastoul. Inflicted with the terrible illness which he wishes to interpret as a sign of grace and not a punishment, meditating on the ways of God, on suffering and on death, excluded from the world of the living while still alive, the poet takes leave of all his friends, one after another, while painting with a black humor the terrible and grotesque traits that would henceforward be his, looking at himself as others would, laughing at himself before others laughed at him. And several years later, as has been seen, Adam de la Halle pushed this dramatization of the self to its logical extreme by writing the *Jeu de la feuillée* as well as his own *Congés*—inspired not by illness, but by his disgust with his native town and its inhabitants. Nowadays, in fact, the *Jeu de la feuillée* is thought to reveal more about the evolution of medieval poetry than it does about that of medieval theater precisely because it is a dramatic work.

Rutebeuf was, however, the ultimate incarnation of this mutation of poetic language. A professional poet who was active between approximately 1250 and 1280, he was born in Champagne but spent his entire poetic career in Paris. He put his pen to work for various causes: the crusades and the defense of the Latin Orient, edifying hagiographic or Marian tales, and, above all, the quarrel between the mendicant orders and the secular masters that took place at the heart of the University of Paris in the 1250s. He also liked to lament his misery. His *dits* (narrative poems) are caricatures of himself and the world produced by a concrete imagination. The poet speaks about himself and claims to tell us about his life and that of his companions in debauchery and misery, even though it would clearly be pointless to try to discover what part, if any, of these false confidences is true: an unhappy marriage, hunger, cold, illness, a degrading bondage to gambling and wine. He likewise recounts his dreams and the allegorical visions with which he claims to have been favored. In the midst of all this, he freely uses jokes, plays on words, and verbal games; he interprets his name by means of fantastic etymologies. In sum, his poetry often gives the impression of being a parade of the self, a theatrical monologue conceived entirely in terms of the effect it will have on the audience, intended to create the impression of unvarnished truth, the improvised product of a mood and discouragement in one of those moments in which all reserve is lost, appearances forgotten, and one can only laugh, sadly or bitterly, at oneself.

Some of the metrical forms he used, like the *tercet coué* (tailed tercet), reinforce the impression of affected offhandedness and weary fluency. Sincerity was in no way a prerequisite for this poetry of everyday things, in contrast to courtly poetry which was nonetheless much more abstract and had rigid formal rules. This poetry aimed simply at a concrete dramatization of the self. It is a poetry of a particular and recognizable reality, but it also travesties this reality and the poetic "I" that describes both this reality and itself.

This definition of the *dit* might lead one to believe that it always contained an element of comedy. This was not at all the case. I have simply chosen examples in which the comic element amplifies the effects produced by the theatrical representation and the exhibition of the self. This theatrical representation and exhibition do not necessarily—in fact they usually do not—take the form of confidences. They are nonetheless always present, if only in the forms of enunciation. As Jacqueline Cerquiglini has written, "the *dit* is a discourse representing an 'I,' it is a discourse in which an 'I' is always represented. The *spoken* text thus becomes the *imitation* of a discourse." Later we will see how late medieval poetry constructed the character of the poet out of a combination of the *dit* and genuinely lyric forms.

The *Fabliaux*

It is neither artificial nor paradoxical to discuss the *fabliaux* in connection with theater and the *dit*. They also presume a type of dramatic performance. Of them, too, one may say that "the *spoken* text becomes the *imitation* of a discourse." They, too, eagerly exhibit the "I" who articulates them. And the tavern, misery, and laughter are everywhere. Their common atmosphere and effects create a relation between the three forms. Their authors, when we know them, are often the same (Jean Bodel, Rutebeuf, Jean de Condé). In medieval terminology itself, finally, the borders of the *dit* and the *fabliau* are not always well marked.

The *fabliaux* are, in the words of Joseph Bédier, "comic tales in verse."[1] They were immensely successful at the end of the thirteenth century and the beginning of the fourteenth. About 150 texts, most of them a couple hundred lines long, are generally identified as *fabliaux*. They were ordinarily written in octosyllabic couplets with a few interesting exceptions, like *Richeut*, the oldest of them, and the *Prêtre qui fut mis au lardier* (*The Priest Who Was Put in the Larder*), whose meter is lyric. Their subjects are traditional and conventional, and some of them lend themselves to moral lessons. They may be found in the folklore of many countries as well as in edifying compilations, even in the Middle Ages—like the *Disciplina clericalis* (*Clerical Discipline*) of the converted Spanish Jew, Pierre Alphonse—in collections of *exempla*, in fables, and in animal stories. This very universality makes hypotheses concerning the genesis of the genre uncertain. The key to the plot is generally a deception that makes us laugh at the character who is deceived, often a trickster who is tricked. Sometimes, however, the situation is pungent without really being comic, and the lesson it teaches is perfectly serious (*La pleine bourse de sens* [*The Full Purse of Sense*], *La housse partie* [*The Shared Cover*]).

There are a great many stories of deceived husbands, of lewd priests, and mutilated seducers. About a third of the *fabliaux* are scatalogical or obscene, to the point that the crudity of the expression and the scabrousness of the situations often astonish even those of us who are not particularly prudish. Such *fabliaux* include *Le Chevalier qui faisait parler les cons et les culs* (*The Knight Who Made Cunts and Asses Speak*)—the ancestor of the *Bijoux indiscrets* (*Indiscreet Jewels*), but without the euphemism—*Le Prêtre crucifié* (*The Crucified Priest*), *Le Rêve des vits* (*The Dream of the Cocks*), *Les trois dames qui trouvèrent un vit* (*The Three Ladies Who Found a Cock*), *Le sot chevalier* (*The Stupid Knight*), *La Demoiselle qui ne pouvait entendre parler de foutre* (*The Young Lady Who Couldn't Stand to Hear Talk about Fucking*), *La Crotte* (*The Turd*), *Le Pet au vilain* (*The Peasant's Fart*), and many others. This insistent indecency has intrigued scholars and given rise to widely varying analyses and interpretations.[2]

---

[1] J. Bédier, *Les Fabliaux* (Paris: Champion, 1893).
[2] Compare, for example, R. H. Bloch, *The Scandal of the Fabliaux* (Chica-

Perhaps there is some relation between the sensuality of courtly poetry, permitting itself everything except an explicit reference to the pudenda, and the obscenity of the *fabliaux*, which, on the contrary, when they speak of love, consider only those parts of the body that are directly involved. One might thus take into account the two opposing aspects of "the courtly neurosis."[1]

This vulgarity and indecency, joined to the genre's general tone and flatfooted cynicism, have led some scholars to doubt that the *fabliaux* could have been intended for the same public as the courtly romances. Joseph Bédier, for example, considered the *fabliaux* to be "the poetry of the common people."[2] This opposition has no basis, however. As Per Nykrog has shown, the public was the same for all these literary genres, and the opposition between courtliness and "realism" is only one of stylistic conventions.[3] This is why it makes sense to interpret the two modes of expression in relation to one another.

The subjects and the spirit of certain *fabliaux* reappeared in the *nouvelles* and the comic theater of the late Middle Ages, but the genre itself died out in the first third of the fourteenth century.

The *Roman de Renart*

The overlap between the *fabliaux* and animal stories was noted earlier. Both provoke laughter or a smile and may serve as vehicles for moral lessons. The Middle Ages had its share of animal fables, but they tended to converge, during the heyday of the *fabliaux*, around the *Roman de Renart* (*Romance of Renart*).

The Middle Ages knew Aesop only by name. They used this name, however, to designate the genre of the fable: the *isopet*. Phaedrus's collection of Latin verse tales, still known in the

---

go: Univ. of Chicago Press, 1986); P. Menard, *Les Fabliaux, contes à rire du Moyen Age* (Paris: Presses Universitaires de France, 1983); C. Muscatine, *The Old French Fabliaux* (New Haven: Yale Univ. Press, 1986); and M. Schenck, *The Fabliaux: Tales of Wit and Deception* (Amsterdam: Benjamins, 1987).

[1] This is the title of a book: H. Rey-Flaud, *La Névrose courtoise* (Paris: Navarin, 1983).

[2] J. Bédier, *Les Fabliaux* (Paris: Champion, 1893).

[3] P. Nykrog, *Les Fabliaux: Etude d'histoire littéraire et de stylistique médiévale*, 2d edn. (Geneva: Droz, 1973).

ninth century, was subsequently lost until the end of the six-teenth century. But the fables of his late imitator, Flavius Avi-anus, survived, and new Latin compilations and adaptations appeared in the tenth century: the *Esope d'Adémar* (*Book of Fables of Adémar*), copied by Adémar de Chabannes, and the *Esope de Wissembourg* (*Book of Fables of Wissembourg*), both in prose, and especially the *Romulus*, which claims to be a transla-tion from Greek that a certain Romulus made for his son Tiber-nius, and which existed in both prose and verse versions. The Latin prose *Romulus* was exploited or copied, sometimes in an abbreviated form, by many authors, such as Vincent de Beau-vais in the thirteenth century. Several Latin verse adaptations of the *Romulus* were made in the twelfth century, one by Alexan-der Neckham and another attributed to Walter of England. The prose *Romulus* was also augmented—sometimes with the fables of Avianus—in various composite editions. One of these, the *Anglo-Latin Romulus*, was translated into English and was used by Marie de France around 1170 to compose the first collection of fables in French. In the thirteenth and fourteenth centuries, Walter of England's collection was adapted in French in the *Isopet de Lyon* (*Fables of Lyon*) and the *Isopets I et III de Paris* (*First and Third Books of Fables of Paris*), while Alexander Neck-ham's *Novus Esopus* (*New Aesop*) gave birth to the *Isopet II de Paris* (*Second Book of Fables of Paris*) and the *Isopet de Chartres* (*Book of Fables of Chartres*). Avianus's fables were likewise translated into French and known as the *Avionnet*.

The *Roman de Renart* also had Latin antecedents. At the time of Charlemagne, Alcuin wrote a poem entitled *Versus de gallo* (*Poem of the Cock*), and a *Gallus et vulpes* (*The Cock and the Fox*) was composed in the eleventh century. In the tenth or eleventh century, a monk from the monastery of Saint-Evre in Toul wrote the *Ecbasis cujusdam captivi per tropologiam* (*A Moral Tale on the Escape of a Prisoner*), an animal epic in which the animals represent the monks of a monastery. Above all, certain episodes of the *Roman de Renart* first appeared in the *Ysengri-mus*, a 6,500-line poem written around 1150—one hundred fifty years before the oldest known branch of the *Roman de Renart*—and attributed for a long time to a monk of Ghent named Nivardus. Nivardus's fox is named Reinardus, his wolf Ysengrimus. The relation to the characters of the *Roman* is obvious. A long debate about these texts, roughly analogous to that concerning the *chansons de geste*, has opposed those who refuse, most improbably, to accept that the *Roman de Renart* had any sources other than Latin ones and those who emphasize, sometimes clumsily, the universal proliferation of animal stories and their often oral diffusion.

The *Roman de Renart* is not a seamless and homogeneous composition. It is made up of a certain number of independent parts, or branches, written by different authors and united by the weakest of narrative links. The oldest part has traditionally been called the second branch, and was composed around 1175 by Pierre de Saint-Cloud. It recounts Renart's misadventures with Chantecler the cock, the titmouse, Tibert the cat (the trap), and Tiécelin the crow (the fox and the crow); it then goes on to describe Renart's visit to Hersent the she-wolf, the treatment he inflicts on the wolf-cubs, and the rape of Hersent at Maupertuis. Starting at the end of the twelfth century, a whole series of continuations were added to this branch. Branch I is the logical and chronological sequel to Branch II, but comes first in all the manuscripts (the judgement of Noble the lion; the siege of Maupertuis; and Renart the dyer). Branches Va (another complaint by Isengrin before Noble; Renart's oath on the body of Roonel the dog), Vb (Renart, Isengrin, and the ham; Renart and Frobert the cricket), and XV (Renart, Tibert, and the chitterlings) are likewise grafted directly onto Branch II. The other early branches are III (the eels; Isengrin's fishing), IV (Renart and Isengrin in the well), and XIV (Renart and Primaut). The Alsatian poet Heinrich der Glîchezaere wrote a coherent and complete account of the adventures of Renart entitled *Reinhart Fuchs (Reinhart the Fox)* as early as 1190, and yet other branches were composed throughout the thirteenth century.

Diverse social categories, whose behavior was reflected in that of their animal incarnations, were chided in the authors' gleeful exercise of their talent: the king Noble, the great feudal lords represented by Isengrin and his friends, the clergy represented by the ass Bernard. Certain branches of the *Roman de Renart* play on the ambiguous, sometimes animal, sometimes human, nature of the characters. Renart pays a gallant visit to Hersent, as a courtly lover would his lady. But he "compisse" ("pisses all over") the wolf cubs, falling back into animality, and the castle again becomes a den. Pursued by Isengrin and Hersent, he takes refuge in his castle of Maupertuis. But this castle is itself a fox's burrow, in whose too narrow entrance—the *mal pertuis*, or bad hole—the she-wolf gets stuck, and the fox, leaving by another exit, takes advantage of the situation (*a tergo more ferarum*). The gait of Grimbert the badger is evoked in a way that is realistic, but is also comical if one imagines a man waddling like a badger. Renart mounts a horse to go to Noble's court, but this horse dawdles and falters because its master is in no hurry to arrive, and one soon perceives that it has no other hoofs than the paws of the fox. The funeral cortege of Lady Coppée, the hen, is described in an altogether human fashion, but the deceased deserves to be mourned, we are told, because she "laid big eggs"; and Chantecler, who leads the mourners, "beats his palms" as he walks along, like a man who wrings his hands—or like a cock who beats his wings. At other points beasts and humans have complex relationships. The former remain subject to their habits and their condition, but they are wild and predatory animals, as well as barons in the animal kingdom, and they are confronted with humans who always belong to the lower classes of society (peasants or humble country priests). The relation of beast to human is thus often that of aristocrat or lord, whose demands and brutality the animals embody, to serf. Everywhere, finally, the ambiguity of the mask is at play: is one dealing with animals dressed up like humans or with humans dressed up like animals?

Despite its acerbity, the *Roman de Renart* is not in itself a work of social or political satire, but it was used in this way. Rutebeuf's *Renart le bestourné* (*Renart Upside Down*, 1261), the *Couronnement de Renart* (*Coronation of Renart*, between 1263 and 1270), and, to a far greater degree, Jacquemart Giélée's *Renart le nouvel* (*The New Renart*, around 1288), and the encyclopedic *Renart le contrefait* (*The Imitation Renart*, between 1320 and 1340) take up the figure of Renart and the framework provided by his adventures in order to introduce, in Rutebeuf's case, a political satire or, in the case of the other works, a polemical review of the estates and the state of the world. With a sort of amused and cynical detachment, the *Roman de Renart* maintains an equal balance between Renart and his adversaries, depicting them as equally despicable and odious. Later, the weight of condemnation often falls entirely on the fox. He is the incarnation of evil, symbolized by his reddish color, and his enemies the incarnation of good. In the *Roman de Fauvel* (*Romance of Fauvel*, 1310–1316), Fauvel is a mythical animal who represents all the baseness and hypocrisy of the world—the powerful argue over the honor of wiping his bottom—and is likewise characterized, as his name indicates (*fauve* = reddish brown), by the tawny color of his coat. Except for the *Roman de Renart*, medieval animal stories all tend towards moralization, whether they are *isopets* or works like Ramon Lull's *Livre des bêtes* (*Book of the Beasts*), inspired by 'Abd Allah Ibn al-Muqaffa''s *Kalīla wa-Dimna* (*Calila and Dimna*).

The genres presented in this chapter are characterized by the dramatic exhibition of the self, and by satire and laughter. They perhaps also have one further point in common: their reflection of the urban spirit of the thirteenth century. For the hierarchical order of the castle and the seigniorial court, for the courtly ideal, they substituted intertwining streets, the sharing and contestation of power, a disillusioned depiction of the ways of the world, the display of human misery. Not, it bears repeating, because they had their own particular authors and audiences, but because, with them, the entire literary universe changes. Their authors were from Arras (from Jean Bodel to Adam de la Halle), from Paris (Rutebeuf), from Lille (Jacquemart Giélée), from Troyes (the anonymous author of *Renart le contrefait*); and these works are haunted by the spirit of the town.

8 *Allegory*

Medieval Allegory: Rhetoric and Exegesis

Allegory was an essential element of medieval literature and, more fundamentally, of medieval thought. In the realm of French letters, it found its consummate expression at the heart of the thirteenth century in the *Roman de la Rose* (*Romance of the Rose*), whose repercussions were immense and long-lasting. Allegory no longer holds the same fascination for us. We find it thin and monotonous. But this is because we understand it poorly, influenced as we are by a modern distinction between allegory and symbolism that works to its detriment. This distinction does not correspond at all to medieval categories. The only distinction made in the Middle Ages reserved the word *symbol* for theology—in which, according to John Duns Scotus, it refers to a type of allegory—whereas the word *allegory*, even though it belonged to the vocabulary of exegesis, entered the literary field through its use in rhetoric. Before one can begin the study of medieval allegorical literature, then, one must forget one's notions about allegory.

Allegory was defined in two ways in antiquity. One of these, first Aristotle's and then Quintillian's, belonged strictly to rhetoric: allegory is a prolonged metaphor, a chain of metaphors. The other, more common, definition was generally current in the Middle Ages. It held that allegory is a trope through which one understands one thing by another, or, in other words, a trope through which one means something other than what one says. This was the definition of Heraclitus, and it was taken over by Saint Augustine, Isidore of Seville, the Venerable Bede, and many others. More than the first, purely grammatical, definition, this one was sensitive to the hermeneutic value of allegory. It is thus in accord with the principal use of allegory in the Middle Ages as an essential method of exegesis.

Everything encouraged the medieval reader to seek a second meaning in Holy Scripture: Christ's parables, his own interpretation of the parable of the Sower, the constant invitation in the New Testament to prefer the spirit over the letter, Christianity's natural tendency to discover a prophetic announcement or prefiguration of the coming of Christ or of the redemption in all the books of the Old Testament and in the entire history of the Hebrew people. In the patristic period, under the influence of Origen, Saint Jerome, and Saint Augustine, this search for a second meaning was formalized and constituted the kernel of the exegetical process. From this time on, each passage of Scripture was held to have four meanings: a literal or historical meaning; an allegorical or spiritual meaning; a tropological or moral meaning; and an anagogic or eschatological meaning. In the Middle Ages, the anagogic meaning tended to be confused with the allegorical one and scholars were often content to consider only the first three levels of meaning. Both sermons and university commentaries on the Bible were often organized around the successive elucidation of these three meanings, although they sometimes dealt only condescendingly, or even mistrustfully, with the literal meaning and historical exegesis. They privileged the two other levels of meaning, both second or allegorical meanings in the broad sense of the term.

From the professor of theology to the simple believers who listened week after week to the Sunday sermon, people in the Middle Ages were used to looking for a second meaning behind the letters or beneath the surface. Humankind had been created in the image of God and all cosmology consisted of correspondences. As Bernard Silvester explained in his twelfth-century *Cosmographia (On Cosmogony)*, the macrocosm, or universe, was reflected in the microcosm, or human being. Not only texts (*allegoria in verbis*, or allegory in words), but events (*allegoria in factis*, or allegory in events) called for an allegorical interpretation. A second, spiritual, meaning referring prophetically to the Revelation was assumed to exist even in the works of certain pagan authors. In order to illustrate the meaning of the word *allegoria*, for example, Isidore of Seville proposed two allegorical interpretations of Virgil. In northern Italy, around 970, a grammarian named Vilgardo pushed this idea to the point where it toppled over into heresy. But no one criticized Bernard Silvester for his allegorical commentary on the *Aeneid*.

It is thus not surprising that medieval scholars and authors were not content simply to interpret allegorically Scripture, the world, and the literature of earlier periods, but themselves produced a great many literary works intended to be read for the sake of their "higher" meanings.

Allegory and Personification before the *Roman de la Rose*
Antiquity offered numerous examples of personification, which, while it is far from being the sum of literary allegory, does play an essential role in it. The pagan gods themselves were often the personifications of concrete realities or abstract notions. And already in the work of Homer, their struggles around the hero are sometimes close to being a reflection of the inner trouble agitating him. Even much later, however, in the works of Virgil or Statius, for example, it is difficult to interpret personifications, however numerous, as purely literary ornaments once religion has made them real. But in the work of the last great pagan poet, Claudian, at the end of the fourth century, these abstractions are no longer anything more than the actors in a psychomachy, or psychological drama, a "civil war" in the soul between virtues and vices. *Psychomachia* is in fact the title of a work by the roughly contemporary Christian, Prudentius: in accordance with a plan that was to have a great future, Prudentius described the combat between Faith and Idolatry, Chastity and Libido, Humility and Pride, and so on. The pagan Martianus Capella's *De nuptiis Philologiae et Mercurii* (*The Marriage of Philology and Mercury*) is based entirely on the play of personifications and was immensely successful in the Middle Ages. Adorned by her mother Phronesis (Wisdom) and ready to marry Mercury, Philology is carried up into heaven by Work and Love where she receives as a wedding present the seven liberal arts personified. These seven arts—Grammar, Rhetoric, Dialectic, Arithmetic, Geometry, Astronomy, and Music—formed the basis of instruction in the Middle Ages, and Martianus Capella's work served as a textbook in schools up until the twelfth century.

This century of great intellectual activity and the rediscovery of philosophy also saw the flowering of several Latin works whose speculative ambitions were expressed by means of a concrete argument founded on the representation of personifications. Around 1150, Bernard Silvester's *Cosmographia*, already mentioned above, explained the creation of the world and humankind in accordance with the Platonic cosmogony of the *Timaeus* and the various commentaries on it. This creation is the work of Noys (Divine Thought) and Nature, who, having first created the "macrocosm," go on to create the "microcosm" (i.e., the human being) with the advice of Goodness and the help of Physics. Between 1160 and 1185, Alan of Lille wrote the *De planctu Naturae* (*Complaint of Nature*) and the *Anticlaudianus*. In the first of these works, Nature laments that humankind, made in the image of the macrocosm, has rebelled against her, especially in the matter of love. The title of the second work comes from its desire to trace the portrait of the ideal human being in response to the portrait of the diabolical human being drawn by Claudian in his *In Rufinum* (*Against Rufinus*). It begins with Nature's desire to create a perfect human being with the help of the Virtues. Prudence is sent—in a chariot constructed by the seven Liberal Arts, drawn by the five Senses, and driven by Reason—to request God's aid in this project. Contemplating God in a mirror held by Faith, she requests that he make and hand over to her the human soul, modeling it on his Noys, to which he agrees. Nature makes the body, Concord unites it with the soul, and the Vices, who wish to destroy the new being, are defeated by the Virtues. In a much less ambitious register, Jean de Hanville's *Architrenius* (*Archlamenter*, 1184) relates the hero's voyage in search of Nature through both allegorical places (the palace of Venus, Mount Ambition, and so on) and real ones like the schools and taverns of Paris.

Allegorical poems were first written in French in the first half of the thirteenth century. These works did not continue the reflection on the human being and nature that had been the subject of their Latin predecessors—this was Jean de Meun's innovation when he returned to this subject in the second part of the *Roman de la Rose*. Their tone, rather, was purely moralizing. Around 1215, Raoul de Houdenc's *Songe d'Enfer* (*Dream of Hell*) was the first poem to present its allegorical argument as a dream of its narrator, a convention whose future success was considerable. Raoul's subject likewise had a great vogue: there

were many Ways of Hell and Ways of Paradise throughout the
thirteenth century and thereafter. Despite abundant personifications, the *Roman de Carité* (*Romance of Charity*) and the *Roman
de Miserere* (*Romance of Miserere*) of Reclus de Molliens (around
1220–1230) are not elaborate allegories. Huon de Méry's
Tournoiement Antéchrist (*Tournament of the Antichrist*), on the
other hand, is perhaps a bit later than the first part of the *Roman de la Rose* (1236?) and presents several innovations as well
as being the narrative of a psychomachy. It includes an Arthurian beginning (the narrator calls forth a messenger of the Antichrist by pouring water on the curb-stone of the spring of
Barenton, as in Wace's and Chrétien's romances); a reflection,
already present in Alan of Lille's *De planctu*, on good and bad
love; a debate of amorous casuistry; and finally, a strongly
autobiographical flavor. The narrator, moreover, is not content
simply to watch the fight between the Virtues and the Vices; he
is wounded by an arrow that Venus shoots at Chastity, and as
a result of this wound, ends his days as a monk.

All these poems claim to relate an experience, a vision, or a
dream of the narrator. They thus situate themselves in the
perspective of the representation of the self that, with the *dit*,
defined the new orientation of poetry in the thirteenth century,
as we saw in the preceding chapter. These poems prepared the
transition from a psychomachy's general depiction of the movements of the soul to a particular confession of a unique individual experience. This was the tendency of allegorical poetry right
through to the end of the Middle Ages. But, still in the thirteenth century, a highly unusual work influenced all allegorical
literature in a definitive and profound fashion as well as completely transposing for the first time the Christian allegorical
model into the secular, amorous, and courtly domain.

The *Roman de la Rose*
The *Roman de la Rose* is a poem of more than twenty-two
thousand octosyllabic verses. It was begun around 1230 by
Guillaume de Lorris, who stopped work on the poem at the end
of four thousand lines, and was finished by Jean de Meun
around 1270. It recounts the narrator's conquest of the rose,
representing the young lady he loves, in the form of an allegorical dream. The narrator begins by affirming that contrary to

common opinion, he does not believe that dreams are lies because a dream that he had five years ago has recently been realized. He offers this description of his dream to his lady in the hope that she will be pleased with it. In his dream, he rises one May morning and enters the orchard of Delight which is ruled by Love, surrounded by the virtues whose practice is favorable to it. In the fountain where Narcissus drowned himself, he sees the reflection of a rosebush; he draws nearer, and his attention is drawn to one particularly charming rosebud. At that moment, Love lets fly an arrow that, entering through his eye, strikes his heart. Henceforth, he is in love with the rose and becomes the prisoner of Love, whom he promises to serve. Despite the remonstrances of Reason, and following the advice of Friend, he undertakes the conquest of the rose with the help of Friendly Welcome and in spite of Pride, Jealousy, Bad Mouth, and so on. He obtains a kiss, but Jealousy, warned, builds a castle in which Friendly Welcome is shut up. Guillaume de Lorris's poem breaks off at this point, in the midst of the lover's lamentations, and Jean de Meun takes up the story. After some new vicissitudes—like the intervention of the hypocritical False Seeming, dressed as a Dominican friar, and the corruption of the old duenna who guards Friendly Welcome—and above all after many digressions and discourses, many polemical developments, and many passages touching on the most important philosophical questions, broached from an unexpected angle and in a lively style, the intervention of no one less than Nature herself, assisted by her chaplain Genius (a character borrowed from Alan of Lille), is required before Love's army can take the castle and the narrator can finally—with an indecent precision—deflower the rose before waking.

The presence of the two authors provokes a certain number of questions. We know the first only through the second. Nothing in the first part itself permits us to identify its author or determine its date. In the second part, as Love encourages his men to attack the castle of Jealousy, Jean de Meun has him say that it is right to help Guillaume de Lorris in his amorous quest. Jean thus names his predecessor and, far from supplanting him, makes him the central character of the poem Jean has taken up (lines 10,496–500). Love goes on to prophesy—since, in the argument of the romance, he is a character in the dream

of the narrator, who has now been identified as Guillaume de
Lorris—that Guillaume will write a romance about his adventure. He then cites lines 4,023–28, specifying that they are the
last written by Guillaume, and intimates that he has since died.
He adds:

> Puis vendra Johans Chopinel,
> au cuer jolif, au cors inel,
> qui nestra sur Laire a Meün.
> (10,535–37)

(Then will come Jean Chopinel, of joyous heart and agile
body, who will be born at Meun-sur-Loire.)

This Jean Chopinel, this Jean de Meun, who thus introduces
himself through the voice of Love, will write a continuation of
the romance, he tells us, more than forty years after Guillaume
stops work on it. He is, moreover, not unknown to us. He was
a Parisian clerk who translated some Latin works. At the end of
the 1260s, he seems to have succeeded Rutebeuf as the official
polemicist of the secular masters of the university of Paris in
their struggle with the mendicant orders. Allusions to current
events in his part of the *Roman de la Rose* allow us to date it to
around 1270. If he wrote "more than forty years" after Guillaume, the first part of the *Roman* would date to the years
1225–1230. But is this declaration to be taken literally? "Forty
years" has a symbolic value and may simply represent any long
period of time: the Hebrews, for example, spent forty years in
the desert. This tells us hardly anything more about Guillaume
de Lorris. One might even suspect that Jean de Meun had
invented him did not certain manuscripts contain only the first
part of the romance, or the first part completed by a brief
conclusion that has nothing to do with Jean de Meun's poem.

The perspectives, interests, turns of mind, and tones of the
two poets were very different. They were so different in fact
that Jean de Meun was probably somewhat malicious in so
completely diverting the work of his predecessor under the guise
of fidelity. Guillaume de Lorris was a courtly poet. In its literal-
ism, the plot of his romance is like the narrative development of
the spring stanzas typical of lyric poetry. The faithful service the
lover, Love's prisoner, promises his conqueror according to the

rules of chivalry; the stages of the amorous conquest; the reservations and obstacles he encounters; the qualities of patience, discretion, submission, respect, and elegance his quest requires: all this is very much in keeping with the courtly ideal. The allegorical meaning, moreover, the relation of the signifier to the signified, is elaborated very coherently, as is the prologue's delicate articulation of the consciousness of the dreamer, that of the poet, his memories, and his hopes; and of the time of the dream, the season and the hour of the day in the dream, the time of memory, the time of writing, the time, hinted at, of the maturation of the real love—five years later, the narrator recalls the dream he had when he was twenty, the age at which Love "levies a toll on young people" (21–23), recalls it at the moment when real love has finally elucidated the meaning of the dreamt love. Guillaume de Lorris also wished to write an art of love. He remembered Ovid, but he also undoubtedly remembered the habitual didacticism of allegorical poetry. If one asks the title of the romance he is writing, he says,

> Ce est li *Romanz de la Rose*,
> ou l'art d'Amors est tote enclose.
> (36–37)

(It is the *Romance of the Rose*, in which the whole art of love is contained.)

An art of love: this is also the way Jean de Meun defines his work through the voice of Love, but in rather different terms:

> Tretuit cil qui ont a vivre
> devroient apeler ce livre
> le *Miroër aus Amoreus*.
> (10,619–21)

(In the future, everyone should call this book the *Mirror for Lovers*.)

A mirror, as was remarked above, is a compendium, an encyclopedia. Jean de Meun was a man of his times; he had a taste for a totalizing knowledge. The narrative argument and the allegorical construction that he inherited from his predecessor, and treated flippantly, were for him an excuse to talk about everything, in an apparent disorder that, as we will see, is deceiving. He not only includes very long digressions, sometimes one inside another, spoken by a jealous husband or an old match-maker giving advice on how to seduce a lady, he also introduces scientific and philosophical discourses (on cosmology, for example, or the courses of the stars and the question of their influence on human destiny); polemical perfidies (on the hypocrisy of the mendicant orders); expositions and explanations of various myths (of Fortune, Adonis, Pygmalion, and the Golden Age); examples borrowed from current events; and discussions of, or reflections on, the most debated topics of his time or topics preoccupying him. These topics include the controversy over universals (concerning the nature of general ideas and the necessary or arbitrary relation of words to them); the nature and value of women, with both modern and classical examples, from Lucretia to Héloïse; the appearance of property and social hierarchies, which brought about the dissolution of the Golden Age; and, of course, the nature and laws of love.

His opinions on this last point—or, rather, the opinions he puts in the mouths of his characters, for he never expresses an opinion in his own name—are not at all courtly: one must obey nature in all things and satisfy the sexual instinct, the gage of fertility, which it has given us. Fidelity is a delusion: Nature did not create Robin for Marion alone or Marion for Robin alone, but "all women for all men and all men for all women." The change the rose undergoes in the second part of the *Roman* is a telling sign of this rupture with Guillaume de Lorris's values. In Guillaume's part of the poem, the rose represents the woman he loves; in Jean's part, it represents only her sexual organs, while the young lady herself tends to be identified with Friendly Welcome, who in Guillaume de Lorris's system represented only that aspect of the young lady favorable to the lover. Love, who is all powerful in Guillaume's part of the poem, is thus subject to Nature and Reason in Jean de Meun's, an apology for a hedonism claiming to be founded on the divine order, confused here with nature.

Through irony and subversion, Jean de Meun leads his predecessor's work down roads it never wished to take. The poem's apparent confusion dissimulates a sort of rigorous dialectic progression: Nature and Genius cannot preach the truth of natural love until all the characters—Friend, the Old

Woman, False Seeming—have exposed the artificiality and essential hypocrisy of courtly love, directly, indirectly, or by antiphrasis.

Guillaume de Lorris's elegant effortlessness, the skill with which he retains all the value and concrete seductiveness of the signifier without blurring the second meaning; Jean de Meun's intellectual force, his depth, his verve, the density of his style: the *Roman de la Rose* was lucky to have two authors who were so remarkable as well as so different.

The Influence of the *Roman de la Rose*
The *Roman de la Rose* was prodigiously successful. While the immense majority of medieval works in French are preserved in fewer than ten manuscripts, many of them in only one or two, we know of more than 250 manuscripts of the *Roman*. Jean de Meun's polemical spirit, provocative opinions, and blatant misogyny gave rise to a "quarrel of the *Roman de la Rose*" at the end of the fourteenth century and beginning of the fifteenth, a quarrel engaging such figures as Jean Gerson, Christine de Pizan, Jean de Montreuil, and Gontier and Pierre Col. But quite aside from this explicit intellectual interest in the questions debated by Jean de Meun, and thanks largely to the *Roman*, allegory became an increasingly important mode of thought and of poetic expression. The allegorical dream, in particular, became a standard convention of both personal and didactic poetry. The play between the individual character of a work that claimed to be an autobiographical confidence and the generality of the amorous itinerary sustained fourteenth-century poetry, as we will see shortly. Guillaume de Lorris's characters, especially those embodying the diverse sentiments of the young lady (Friendly Welcome, Pride, Refusal, Shame, Fear) became the shared property of poets and nourished the commonplaces of poetry. The *Roman de la Rose* explicitly inspired King René I d'Anjou's *Livre du cuer d'Amours espris* (*Book of the Heart Inflamed with Love*), which follows it very closely at certain moments. Allegory is constantly hinted at with a fugitive brevity in the poetry of Charles d'Orléans in order to unite spiritual states to the concrete details of life.

Medieval allegory is thus not as redundantly poor as we are too ready to believe. Its capacity to bring to light the correspondences structuring the universe and to express psychic realities too obscure or too upsetting to be easily named or directly analyzed gives it a hermeneutic value. Allegory becomes dry, confined to the role of literary ornament, only when modern thought—more sensitive to distinctions and oppositions than correspondences, more attentive to causes than to meanings—denies it this value.

PART FOUR
THE END OF THE MIDDLE AGES

The last two centuries of the Middle Ages are always treated as a separate, dying world. Scholars speak of them as the "decline" or the "autumn" of the Middle Ages. Johan Huizinga's famous book on the subject was published in French under these two titles successively.[1] This period was marked by singularly serious political, social, and religious crises: the Hundred Years' War; rebellions in the towns of Flanders, in Paris and Rouen; the *Jacquerie* or peasants' revolt in France, and the Peasant's Revolt in England; the collapse of feudal values no longer compatible with the centralization of power and the birth of a national spirit; the malaise of a knighthood unable to evolve militarily or socially; inflation—a new affliction—and the "changes of fortune" it brought with it; the plague, which depopulated Europe; the last hurrahs of the crusades and the disaster of Nicopolis; the Great Schism of the West; and the religious movements that were the forerunners of the Reformation—the Lollards in England and later the Hussites in Bohemia. These crises of course had repercussions in the domain of culture understood in the broadest sense: debauchery, anxiety, apocalyptic prophecy, perverted manifestations of religious sentiment (flagellants, organized massacres), a bloody theatricalization of behavior, and an unbridled taste for luxury. But it is too often and too easily assumed that this set of crises brought about a literary decadence. In reality, it is just as likely that literature will be nourished by crises as suffer from them. Italy experienced the same crises as the rest of Europe in the fourteenth

---

[1] Johan Huizinga, *Le Déclin du Moyen Age*, trans. J. Bastin (Paris: Payot, 1932); *L'Automne du Moyen Age*, trans. J. Bastin, new edn. (Paris Payot, 1975). The English title is *The Waning of the Middle Ages: A Study of the Forms of Life, Thought and Art in France and the Netherlands in the XIVth and XVth Centuries*, trans. F. Hopman (London: Arnold, 1924).

century and was nonetheless in the midst of its Renaissance. One must not appeal to uncertain chains of causes and effects in order to shore up the commonplaces that later gained acceptance—for very particular reasons and in very particular circumstances—among the poets of the French Renaissance.

In several domains, nonetheless, French literature of the fourteenth and fifteenth centuries did go in directions that had no future. It is only our awareness of this future sterility, however, that fills us, retrospectively, with a foreboding of decline with respect to movements then full of vigor. Had the gaudy, flamboyant Burgundian world triumphed in the fifteenth century, the subsequent evolution of French letters would perhaps have been very different and we would perhaps look at the literature of this period from a very different point of view.

9   *Poetry in the Fourteenth and Fifteenth Centuries*

The New Rules of the Lyric Game

The poetry of the late Middle Ages, so despised by the Renaissance, was the most prestigious literary genre of its day. "At the time of Guillaume de Machaut," Daniel Poirion has written, "one can say that lyricism constituted the hard kernel of literary production."[1] Poetry expanded and diversified, while the spread of prose and its growing monopoly on narrative forms tended by opposition to provide all verse production with a unity it had not previously possessed. The notion of poetry that had emerged in the thirteenth century came to cover everything written in verse. And because verse was considered more ornate and difficult than prose, it was also thought to be more literary, so to speak. This was the source of its special prestige. Prose writers, inversely, prided themselves on the greater truthfulness of their work, but recognized, albeit not without a certain self-satisfaction, that it was less sophisticated than that of the poets. The true man of letters began to be called the *poet*—the word appears for the first time with something like its modern meaning at the end of the thirteenth century in the *Livre du trésor* (*Book of Treasure*) an encyclopedia written in French by the Florentine Brunetto Latini. As *chansons de geste* and verse romances became so rare that they seemed no more than antiquarian exercises, verse, the object of the new notion of poetry, became more and more clearly associated with the expression of feelings and the depiction of the self that characterized, albeit in a different and almost contrary fashion, both courtly lyricism and the *dit*.

---

[1] D. Poirion, *Le Poète et le prince: L'évolution du lyrisme courtois de Guillaume de Machaut à Charles d'Orléans* (Paris: Presses Universitaires de France, 1965).

As it expanded in the fourteenth century, then, poetry combined a genuinely lyric esthetic with that of the *dit*. The *dit* provided a semi-narrative frame and an autobiographical point of departure. Lyric pieces were easily inserted into this frame, where they played the role of an emotional commentary. At the same time, the increasing recourse to fixed poetic forms turned these lyric pieces in upon themselves and made them independent poems. The frame provided by the *dit* was eventually erased and the lyric pieces, left to themselves, were organized into collections in order to create an illusion of continuity, indeed of narrative. Thus Guillaume de Machaut, in his *Voir dit* (*True* dit) tells how he, an aging and famous poet, received a letter from a very young female admirer, how there arose between them a poetic and sentimental correspondence, and how love led them beyond correspondence. The *dit* contains both letters and poems. Machaut had already used a comparable structure twenty years earlier in his *Remède de Fortune* (*Remedy for Fortune*). Jean Froissart's *Espinette amoureuse* (*Amorous Hawthorn*) likewise evokes the young poet's loves, and one could cite many more examples. The collections of lyric pieces sought more than just formal unity by restricting themselves to a single form (like the ballad) or by defining themselves through a round number of poems (like the *Cent ballades* [*Hundred Ballads*] of Christine de Pizan or Jean le Seneschal, or the *Cinquante ballades* [*Fifty Ballads*] John Gower wrote in French); they presumed that each poem was a moment in a story whose plot remained implicit but which the lyric commentary permitted one to guess or to reconstruct. Such collections include Machaut's *Louange des dames* (*Praise of Ladies*), Christine de Pizan's *Cent ballades d'amant et de dame* (*Hundred Ballads of Lover and Lady*), or even, as we will see, the poems of Charles d'Orléans as he arranged them in his own manuscript.

Lyric poems abandoned the long, free form of the *canso* (song), which united the story and the cry of a love. Henceforth, the story was taken over by the *dit* or by the collection seen now as a genre of composition. For lyricism itself there remained the cry, expressed in fixed poetic forms, coiled around their refrains.

This coiling was felt so strongly that the name *rondeau* (little round) was no longer attributed to the *ronde* (round), the dance in a circle that had perhaps given it its name and defined its form, but to the form itself, felt to be a circular form, a round form, a form, it was written, "that turns back on itself like a circle, beginning and ending in the same way." Poets systematically exploited its most striking traits: the contrasting voices of the refrain and the stanza, the echo, the discontinuity, the sketchiness. Sensitive to the importance of the refrain, Guillaume de Machaut tended to privilege it over the stanza. One thus awaits its arrival all the more impatiently and feels its impact all the more strongly because it comes after the filler-verses of a banal stanza. Other poets emphasized the circular movement of the *rondeau* by stripping their texts to the bone in order to show that this movement alone was enough to give poetic density to a transparent text, and to create an illusion of simplicity, a melancholy stiffness that would later be attributed to "popular" songs. This is the style of certain of Eustache Deschamps's and Christine de Pizan's *rondeaux* and it contrasts strongly with these poets' habitual style. Sometimes, however, the *rondeau* overflowed its very short original pattern (*ABaBabAB*: a two-line refrain, a verse, a one-line refrain, two verses, a two-line refrain). It could expand to several stanzas, and both the refrain and the stanza could be lengthened. Its refrain, moreover, whether internal or final, could be reduced to a single line. This seems to have been the case often in the poetry of Charles d'Orléans, insofar as his refrains can be reconstructed on the basis of a manuscript tradition that systematically provides only their first words. This method of writing suggests a new way of reading that allowed one to peruse the poem for its novelties without being forced to listen to its repetitions, merely leaving the door open to their possible return. The *rondeau* survived a long time with a refrain thus reduced to a half line or even to a single word.

Other genres more easily and more naturally provided the length required by a flamboyant rhetoric. The *virelai* met this requirement only halfway. The second part of its two-part stanza repeated the rhyme scheme of the refrain, which thus served as both prelude and finale to each stanza (*AbbaA*). This genre was thus very similar to the *rondeau*, save that it had no internal refrain. The role of the refrain was all the more important because the second part of the stanza shared its structure:

if the stanza was to be substantial, the refrain had to be substantial as well. In principle, every reduction of the repetitive portion of the poem was matched by a comparable reduction of its discursive portion. Poets often sought to make the *virelai* the vehicle of a detailed analysis of feelings. Deschamps and Christine de Pizan, whose *rondeaux* were so different, both forced it into the service of a didactic or simply intellectual poetry for which it was ill-suited. Here again the repetition of the refrain was eventually curtailed because it had become a limitation.

In these conditions, the success of forms in which the refrain was relatively short, like the ballad, or in which there was no refrain, like the *chant royal* (royal song), is not surprising. Coming at the end of each of the three stanzas and the envoi of the ballad, its one-line refrain pleases the mind like an apt quotation, ingeniously adapted each time to the context, rather than moving the senses through dizzying rhythms and echoes. At the same time, the regularity and length of the meter—the decasyllable is the verse form most often used by the ballad and the *chant royal*—enabled the poetic discourse to spread itself out and display its articulations. It is easy to understand also how collections of ballads could be composed to suggest a narrative, one that could be sustained, moreover, by a *dit*.

Its separation from music is a final, but essential, trait marking the late medieval lyric. Guillaume de Machaut, who in the *Voir dit* portrayed his young female admirer as capable of rhyming but not of "making notes," was the last poet-musician. His "nephew," Eustache Deschamps, was not able to compose music and dissociated musical composition from the art of poetry in his *Art de dictier et de faire chansons* (*Art of Versifying and Making Songs*, 1392), the first treatise on French versification. The fixed forms were originally defined as much by their music as by their meter—and were thus linked to dance, as the names of the *rondeau* and the ballad indicate—but they gained a new importance, paradoxically, when they were no longer sung. This separation from music brought with it a new attention to prosody and to the virtuoso effects it made possible, as is shown in the work of the *grands rhétoriqueurs*, or "great rhetoricians," of the fifteenth century. The *canso*, on the other hand, became a simple song. Two sumptuous manuscripts of the fifteenth century collected a number of songs with a "popular" bent, many preserving, albeit in a simplified manner, the form of the earliest courtly lyricism.

Guillaume de Machaut and His Heirs

Guillaume de Machaut dominated the poetry of the fourteenth century. He was a native of Champagne, born around 1300. After studies leading to at least a Master of Arts degree, he entered the service of Jean de Luxembourg, king of Bohemia, around 1323, and in 1337, King Jean obtained a canonry at Reims for him from the pope. Shortly thereafter, he left his first patron and entered the service of Jean's daughter, Bonne de Luxembourg, the wife of Jean, duke of Normandy, who later became King Jean II le Bon of France. When Bonne died in 1349, Machaut attached himself to the king of Navarre, Charles d'Evreux, who was later called "le Mauvais" ("the Bad"). After 1357, Machaut was in the service of Jean, duke of Berry, although he was also in close contact with Jean's older brother Charles, duke of Normandy and later king of France (Charles V), at whose court he stayed and whom he received at his house in Reims. He died there in April 1377.

Machaut's career indicates the importance of patronage at the end of the Middle Ages. Courts imposed their fashions and attracted the most famous writers. In the fifteenth century, the writers of the Burgundian court were true court officials. The practice and even the nature of poetry were profoundly influenced by the relations between the poet and the prince, as is suggested by the title of Daniel Poirion's fundamental work.[1]

I will leave aside here Machaut's important musical works like his famous *Messe* (*Mass*) and his twenty-some motets. His literary *oeuvre* includes some four hundred lyric pieces, a dozen *dits*, of which the *Voir dit* (1364) is the last and by far the longest, and a long historical poem, the *Prise d'Alexandrie* (*Capture of Alexandria*), devoted to the life of the king of Cyprus, Pierre I de Lusignan. Towards the end of his life, he composed a *Prologue* to his collected works containing both an art of poetry and something of an art of living in verse.

To the courtly inspiration, allegorical frame, and imagery

---

[1] D. Poirion, *Le Poète et le prince*.

inherited from the *Roman de la Rose* (in his *Fontaine amoureuse* [*Amorous Spring*] for example), and the theatricalization of the self inherited from the *dit*, Machaut added the interests and accents of his time, interests and accents one finds even more clearly in the work of his successors: an attention to time, to dates, and to aging, and a new relation to reality. The poet who evoked the calamities of his day—the plague, flagellants, the massacre of Jews—in the introduction to the debate of amorous casuistry forming his *Jugement du roi de Navarre* (*Judgement of the King of Navarre*); the poet who consoled this same king of Navarre as he languished in the prisons of the king of France, in the *Confort d'Ami* (*Friend's Comfort*); the poet who transformed a difference in ages and an awareness of the time and the stages of a relationship into the charm and drama of the *Voir dit*: this poet managed to engage poetry in a kind of dialogue with reality that had long eluded it, without forcing it to reflect this reality, while simultaneously and strongly affirming the imperious and independent character of rhetoric and prosody.

These traits, especially the play on the different values of time and the close attention to life, are far more sharply defined in the work of two poets of the following generation who were profoundly influenced by Machaut: Jean Froissart (1337?–after 1404) and Eustache Deschamps (1346–1406). I will have a great deal more to say later about Froissart as a chronicler. His career as a recognized and celebrated man of letters, protected by a succession of patrons and, like Machaut, endowed by one of them with a canonry, is not without other similarities to Machaut's. Deschamps, Froissart's contemporary, was, like Machaut, from Champagne, and, according to a fifteenth-century tradition, was Machaut's nephew. He interrupted his legal studies and entered the king's service as a messenger. He held diverse administrative positions, like that of the bailiff of Valois, but above all he participated in the joyous, frivolous life of Charles VI's court at the side of the king's brother, Duke Louis d'Orléans, to whom he had been attached since the duke's birth.

Both Froissart and Deschamps acknowledged their debt to Machaut. His allegorical universe and the characters with which he liked to people it (like Fortune) reappeared in their work, especially in Froissart's great poems that give an autobiographical coloring to the allegory (*L'Espinette amoureuse* [*The Amorous Hawthorn*], *Le joli buisson de jeunesse* [*The Pretty Thicket of Youth*]) or are poems of consolation (*La Prison amoureuse* [*The Amorous Prison*]) modeled on Machaut's *Le Confort d'Ami*. Several of Froissart's *dits* were directly inspired by those of the canon of Reims, and Deschamps mourned the death of "Machaut, the noble rhetorician," in a famous ballad. But more than Machaut, Froissart and Deschamps sought to write a poetry of daily life. In one poem, Froissart imagines an argument between his horse and his dog over which one of them suffers the most on the trips their master forces them to take. In the *Dit du florin* (Dit *of the Florin*), he describes his stay at the court of the count of Foix, Gaston Phébus, the sum he received from this prince for reading his romance *Méliador* to him, and the theft of this money during his return trip. Deschamps's enormous and scattered poetic *oeuvre* was nourished even more by the stuff of daily life: a ballad on baldness, a problem shared by several of his noble friends; another recounting a night the king's uncles and some of the greatest lords spent drinking in the infamous cabarets of the capital. Elsewhere the poet complains that the books he lends to people are not returned or relates a comic escapade in Calais while it was occupied by the English. A circumstantial poetry, or a poetry of circumstances— he regularly mentions in the poem the date of its composition.

At Calais, Deschamps was with Oton de Grandson, then in the service of the English, who pretended not to know him while he played the clown and got himself arrested. A nobleman from Savoy with a tragic destiny, Oton was well known in his day for his valor and elegance and was one of the best representatives of the courtly spirit whose dying glow illuminated the end of the fourteenth century. I cannot cite all the poets of this period, but he at least deserves some mention here for his seemingly effortless virtuosity, the fluidity of his poetry, and his elegiac tone.

Christine de Pizan also deserves a special place in the literary history of this period. Born in 1365, daughter of Charles V's Italian astrologer, who brought her with him to France when she was three years old, she was a widow with three children by 1390. From that time until her death around 1430, she supported herself through her writing, fully conscious of the uniqueness, as well as the sorrow, of her situation, always ready to defend the reputation and the condition of women. Her work was abundant and varied because it was written essentially at the request of various patrons. Lyric poetry makes up an important part of it, and posterity has been drawn especially to the simplest pieces mourning the loss of a beloved husband. The influence of Machaut and the quasi-autobiographical, allegorical *dit* is evident, however, in poems like the *Chemin de longue estude* (*Path of Long Study*) and the immense *Livre de mutacion de Fortune* (*Book of Fortune's Change*), whose beginning provides a rather surprising allegory of Christine's life and the drama of her widowhood, after which, she tells us, she changed sex and became a man. The same themes—dream, the intervention of Nature, autobiographical confidences—reappear in her prose *Avision Christine* (*Christine's Vision*). Echoes of the *Roman de la Rose* are naturally very frequent in her work as well, even though she vehemently reproached its misogyny.

The courtly tradition survived into the beginning of the fifteenth century, in the lyric poems of Alain Chartier (c. 1385–1430), for example, notary and secretary to the dauphin, later Charles VII. But the same poet created a scandal with his *Belle Dame sans mercy* (*Beautiful Lady without Pity*, 1424) denouncing the hypocrisy of the courtly game that, in courtly milieux, was no longer anything more than an elaborate masque. As we will see in the next chapter, moreover, his inspiration was far from entirely lyric and amorous.

But fifteenth-century lyric poetry possessed its own character. It was defined above all by two poets, Charles d'Orléans and Villon, and, in its second half, by a number of poets commonly but contestably referred to as the *grands rhétoriqueurs* (great rhetoricians).

Charles d'Orléans

Born in 1394, Charles was the eldest surviving son of Duke Louis d'Orléans, brother of Charles VI, and of Valentina Visconti, daughter of the duke of Milan. He was thirteen when his father was assassinated at the order of his cousin, the duke of Burgundy, Jean Sans-Peur (1407), and twenty-one when he was captured at the battle of Agincourt (1415). He remained a prisoner of the English until 1440. During his captivity, which he spent writing poems—a few of them in English—he lost his second wife, Bonne d'Armagnac, whose father had been the leader of the anti-Burgundian clan ever since the death of Louis d'Orléans. Liberated at last in exchange for an enormous ransom and thanks to the good offices of the duke of Burgundy, Philippe le Bon, he married the very young Marie de Clèves. They had several children, among them the future king of France, Louis XII, born in 1462. After 1451, Charles spent most of his time in retirement at his castle of Blois, writing new poems that he transcribed into the collection of his works he himself copied out around 1450–1455 alongside pieces by the poets whom he gathered around him and those of visitors to Blois: King René d'Anjou, Jean Meschinot, Olivier de la Marche, Georges Chastellain, François Villon. He died on 5 January 1465. He never fulfilled the great political destiny that might have been his, and his life and work remained simultaneously public and secret.

Charles d'Orléans's poetry is clearly of courtly inspiration, especially at the beginning of his career when he wrote under the influence of the faithful Jean de Garancières, devoted knight and poet of the house of Orléans. His *oeuvre* consists mainly of ballads and *rondeaux*. Still heavily influenced by the *Roman de la Rose*, the collection of ballads is introduced by an allegorical verse narrative, the *Retenue d'Amour* (*The Agreement with Love*, 1414), balanced later by the *Songe en complainte* (*Plaintive Dream*, 1437), itself announcing the aging poet's *Departie d'Amour* (*Farewell to Love*). Now and again, the ballads organize themselves into narrative sequences, evoking, for example, the illness and death of the beloved lady. All of Charles d'Orléans's poetry circles around the reflection of time in the self and of the self in time: the weather, conjured up so eagerly by his *rondeaux* ("Yver, vous n'êtes qu'un vilain" ["Winter, you are nothing but a peasant"]; "Le temps a laissé son manteau" ["The season has taken off its coat"]; "En yver, du feu, du feu, / Et en esté, boire, boire" ["In winter, fire, fire, and in summer, drink, drink"]); dates and the seasons (St. Valentine's Day, May Day); passing time and arriving old age; passing life and the prolongation of his imprisonment; small pleasures ("Dîner au bain et souper en bateau" ["Dining in the bath, and supping in a boat"]). It is a "snapshot" poetry that sees each snapshot from the perspective of aging; a poetry in which the self, shaped by its times, is constantly inflected by sadness and its consequence, or its temptation, *nonchaloir*, indifference. It is a poetry, finally, in which the expressions of everyday life ("D'Espoir, et que vous en diroye? / C'est un beau bailleur de parolles" ["And what shall I tell you of Hope? It's a great word-lender"]), sayings ("Petit mercier, petit panier" ["Little clothier, little basket"]), and proverbs give meaning and feeling to—and blunt the grandiloquence of—a skipping, perpetually incomplete allegory: the Forest of Long Waiting, the Book of Thought, Melancholy, Hope, Worry, the dialogue of the Eyes and the Heart. This poetry of everyday life, this poetry of almost nothing, of the first word that comes to mind, written with what seems to be a cheerful and melancholic ease, is most evident in the *rondeaux* and characterizes the final period of the old duke's *oeuvre*, when he was rather annoyed by the pedantic pretentions of the young poets of the new school: "Le monde est ennuyé de moy, / Et moy pareillement de lui" ("The world is tired of me, and I, in turn, of it").

Villon

Villon seems to have visited the court at Blois, and Charles d'Orléans's personal manuscript contains several poems by him. Famous already in his own time—his works were printed as early as 1489, and Clément Marot published a critical edition of them in 1532—he was not entirely, or not only, the marginal figure his poetry, like his encounters with the law, makes him out to be.

His real name was François de Montcorbier. Having lost his father and without resources, he was able to study at the Faculty of Arts in Paris thanks to the generosity of Guillaume de Villon, chaplain of Saint-Benoît le Bétourné. He received his bachelor's degree in 1449 and his master's degree in 1452. After this date, the only definite information we have about him comes from judicial sources. On 5 June 1455, he mortally wounded a priest, Philippe Sermoise, in a brawl. He fled, but returned to Paris after he had received letters of remission from Charles VII in January 1456. On Christmas night in the same year, he and four accomplices—two of whom belonged to the gang known as the Coquillards, whose jargon Villon knew—broke into the Collège de Navarre and stole 500 gold *écus*. Prudently, he then left Paris again. It was probably at this point that he visited the court of Blois and perhaps also the court of Duke Jean II de Bourbon. He spent the summer of 1461 in a prison at Meung-sur-Loire on the order of the bishop of Orléans, Thibaut d'Aussigny, for some unknown infraction. This especially painful experience was the starting point of his *Testament*. Freed on 2 October on the occasion of the recently-crowned Louis XI's entry into the town, he returned to Paris. In November 1462, however, after one of his accomplices confessed, he was arrested for the break-in at the Collège de Navarre, then released after promising to return 120 *écus*. At the end of the same month, he was again imprisoned as the result of a brawl in which a pontifical notary was killed. Sentenced to be hung, he appealed. On 5 January 1463, the Parlement of Paris commuted his sentence to ten years of banishment. Villon again left Paris and we subsequently lose all trace of him.

Except for a few, difficult-to-interpret ballads in the jargon of the Coquillards and a few independent poems linked to his visit to the court of Blois and his encounters with the law, Villon's *oeuvre* consists of two poems in octosyllabic eight-line stanzas, the *Lais* (*Bequests*) and the *Testament*.

The *Lais* (320 lines) claims to be contemporary with the break-in at the Collège de Navarre (Christmas 1456). Alleging an unhappy love affair, Villon announces his intention to leave for Angers and, according to custom, writes a will in case he should not return. In reality, he bequeaths objects he does not possess and his beneficiaries—Parisians from all walks of life—are portrayed in an ironic fashion. Hearing the bell of the Sorbonne ringing the Angelus, he stops writing to pray, and dozes off. When he wakes up, his ink has frozen and his candle has gone out. He thus declares that he is unable to finish his poem. The period of unconsciousness can be interpreted as corresponding to the moment when the theft was committed, and Villon may thus be disclaiming responsibility for his actions in a roundabout fashion.

The *Testament* (186 eight-line stanzas, among which are inserted fifteen ballads, a double ballad, and three *rondeaux*, for a total of 2,023 lines) was composed in 1461–1462, after his imprisonment at Meung. In the first part of the poem, starting from this harsh experience, Villon meditates on his lost youth, his physical and moral decline, his poverty, the sufferings inflicted by love, and death. This meditation is enhanced by ballads (that of the "Dames du temps jadis" ["Ladies of Yesteryear"], for example) interrupting the poem at various points. The second part of the poem is, like the *Lais*, in the form of a testament—in view of approaching death this time, rather than a possible departure—but it is longer, more systematic, and more precise, and its dispositions concerning burial, the distribution of alms, and so on, are in conformity with those of a true testament. The ballads inserted in this part of the poem are written in tribute to the beneficiaries, and are both sincere (a ballad for his mother, for Robert d'Estouteville) and burlesque (a ballad for his "mistress," for Jean Cotart, and so on).

Villon's *oeuvre* was not entirely original. The parodic and fictional testament already existed as a genre, and the "serious" themes he treats were poetic commonplaces. His work is, however, the consummate expression of the ludicrous, mocking, bitter representation of the self that had been inaugurated by the thirteenth-century *dits*. He plays the role of the miserable, depraved, cynical poet with an extreme intensity, cruising the streets of the city, hanging out with prostitutes and delinquents, frequenting bad men and bad places, thinking of nothing but "taverns and women." With extreme audacity, he mixes tones and registers, themes, apparent seriousness and buffoonery, anguish and obscene laughter, allusions and implicit meanings. He subverts courtly love by exaggerating its poses, by cynically blending it with prostitution, by multiplying double entendres. He revitalizes the conventional meditation on death by applying it to those who face it in the most painful and degrading fashion, from torture to scaffold. His fame also owes much to his skillful, fluid, dense versification, to its seductive rhythm and audacious enjambments, and to his sharp feeling for formulas and sayings.

The *Grands Rhétoriqueurs*

The name *grands rhétoriqueurs* (great rhetoricians) is inappropriate and based on a misunderstanding of two lines by Guillaume

Coquillart. But it has become the traditional name for a new tendency found in court poetry from the middle of the fifteenth century to the beginning of the sixteenth. The aged Charles d'Orléans and his entourage refused to accept these innovations, but they flowered at the court of Brittany in the work of Jean Meschinot, at the Bourbon court in that of Jean Robertet, and, above all, at the Burgundian court in that of Michault Taillevent, Georges Chastellain, Olivier de la Marche, Pierre Michault, Jean Molinet, and Jean Lemaire de Belges. During the reign of Charles VIII in the final years of the fifteenth century, this type of poetry flourished at the French court as well, in the work of André de la Vigne, Guillaume Cretin, Octavien de Saint-Gelais, and Jean Marot.

These poets were never united in a "school," but they all shared certain traits. They were court poets, employed and paid by a prince, serving in positions that often had nothing to do with their poetic activity. Their high conception of princely service and the state is evident in their work, which is not limited to lyric poetry, or even to verse. Quick to moralize, anxious to shape opinion for the public good, they paid very little attention to love. In their poems and their poetic treatises (like the *Arts de seconde rhétorique* [*Arts of Second Rhetoric*]), they appealed eagerly to the authority of Alain Chartier, noteworthy both for his taste for political debate and for the blows he had struck against the ideal of courtly love. In general, they renounced fixed poetic forms and wrote longer stanzaic *dits* whose versification was incredibly complex. Their quest for technical virtuosity and verbal prowess in both poetry and prose reveals a constant effort to push the possibilities of language to their extreme limits. Long discredited by the sneerings of the sixteenth-century poets of the Pléiade, this effort has provoked renewed interest in recent years.

10   *The Forms of Reflection: Testimony, Judgement, Knowledge*

War and History

The calamities of the times, the warfare, the conflicts of every kind undoubtedly played their part in the growth of historiography in the fourteenth century, especially in the form of the chronicle, or narrative of one's times. Writers recorded the events of their day because these events captivated them, because no one could escape them, because they were more brutal, more obvious, and more pressing, because they weighed more heavily on the lives of everyone than they had at other times. But the abundance of chronicles also reflects (for what period has not had its burning issues and calamitous events?) the new position of many of the authors in the service of princes and the state. This flowering of historiography was thus also the indirect consequence of the times, the product of the changes brought about by the collapse of the feudal system, the emergence of a national spirit, and the concentration of power in the hands of a prince. These authors had a professional interest in current events and their descriptions of these events were fraught with political intentions. This is true, for example, of the authors who continued the *Grandes Chroniques de France (Great Chronicles of France)* directly in French: Pierre d'Orgemont, who related the reigns of Jean II le Bon (1350–1364) and Charles V (1364–1380), was chancellor of France and made no effort to hide the fact that he was writing for the greater glory of the Valois; Jean Jouvenel des Ursins, author of the history of the reign of Charles VI (1380–1422), was the son of the Jean Jouvenel to whom the king had entrusted the provostship of merchants after the Maillotin uprising, and the brother of the chancellor Guillaume Jouvenel des Ursins. Present at many important events by virtue of their position, heralds also easily became chroniclers. The "héraut Chandos," for example (the herald of the great English captain John Chandos), wrote a *Vie du Prince Noir* (*Life of the Black Prince*) around 1385, to which Cuvelier's *Vie de Bertrand du Guesclin* (*Life of Bertrand du Guesclin*) was—in the "more literary" form of a *chanson de geste*—the French response. The "héraut Berry" (Berry herald), Gilles Le Bouvier, was the author of a *Chronique du roi Charles VII* (*Chronicle of King Charles VII*, 1402–1455)—whose beginning was taken over by the *Grandes Chroniques de France*—a *Histoire de Richard II* (*History of Richard II*, 1440), and a *Recouvrement de Normandie* (*Recovery of Normandy*, 1449). And Jean Lefèvre de Saint Rémy, a Burgundian herald known as Toison d'Or, produced a *Chronique* running from 1408 to 1436. The number of memorialists, anxious to justify their careers and decisions, likewise grew, and I will discuss the most famous of them, Commynes, a bit later. The coloring that writers from the political world or the highest levels of government administration gave to literature extended even beyond the limits of historiography into less likely domains. The *grands rhétoriqueurs* (great rhetoricians) are one example of this influence and we will soon discover other examples at the court of France in the reigns of Charles V and Charles VI.

But, for the fourteenth century, the gigantic mass of Jean Froissart's *Chroniques* is the principal monument of French historiography. We have already met Froissart as a poet. He was born at Valenciennes in the Hainaut region, undoubtedly in 1337. In 1361, he left the Hainaut for England, where he was for eight years the protégé of his compatriot Queen Philippa, the wife of Edward III. During this period he wrote mainly poetry. After the queen's death in 1368, he returned to the Hainaut, where he attracted the patronage of Duke Wenceslas of Brabant, and where in 1373 he finished the first version of the First Book of the *Chroniques* for Robert, count of Namur. He became the parish priest of Estinnes-au-Mont in that same year through the efforts of Gui de Châtillon, count of Blois, who was Froissart's patron as long as fortune permitted, and who later obtained a canonry at Chimay for him. It was at Gui's request that he wrote a second version of the First Book, then a Second Book, and, finally, after a trip to the court of Gaston Phébus, count of Foix and of Béarn, the Third Book of the *Chroniques* (1389). He also began writing his Arthurian verse romance, *Méliador*, in the 1380s. He traveled to England in 1395, but, despite Richard II's friendly welcome, he did not rediscover the world of his youth and so returned disappointed. Back in the Hainaut, he wrote the Fourth Book of the *Chroniques* and rewrote entirely the first part of the First Book. He died sometime after 1404.

Froissart's career was not unlike Machaut's. He was respected and admired at an early age, and his succession of patrons assured him both material security and, thanks to the ecclesiastical benefices, independence. The influence of courts and princely friendships is palpable in Froissart's work, but he was nonetheless a "free-lance" writer and not a court official like his Burgundian successors in the fifteenth century. Having started his career as a poet like Machaut, however, Froissart subsequently devoted most of his energy to the *Chroniques*, which began simply as a compilation and continuation of the *Chroniques* of Jean le Bel, a canon of Liège.

As a chronicler, Froissart has often been judged with undue severity. He has been reproached for his shallowness and lack of political sense, for his preference for spectacle over analysis, for an unthinking adherence to aristocratic prejudices, and for an utterly uncritical fascination with, and admiration for, chivalric pomp and values, whose inconsistency, vanity, and inability to accommodate themselves to the evolution of society, the political game, military art, and, inevitably, hypocrisy, were demonstrated by the very events he related. These criticisms come from a lack of understanding. Froissart sought the meaning of events; and, in order to find it, he used the methods and techniques of the literary genre that was thought to be the most meaningful of all at this time: romance. This is the source of the misunderstanding. The most meaningful aspects and episodes of the *Chroniques* are precisely those most directly inspired by romance. One cannot help but be dumbfounded, moreover, by his efforts and his labor. First of all, his investigative labor: he traveled to England, Scotland, Italy, Béarn, ever seeking to meet people who had witnessed or played a role in events, to gather and compare their testimony. He corrected the "Castilian" version of the events in Spain that he had gathered at the court of Gaston Phébus in 1388–1389, for example, on the basis of information he obtained from the Portuguese Fernando

Pachéco, whom he met the following year in Zeeland. Second, his editorial labor: he wrote several successive versions of the First Book, each one distinguished by a particular perspective, a particular ambition, and particular choices. Indeed, every new copy of the text made under his direction was modified and re-edited with its recipient in mind. He gives us glimpses of this double labor, portraying himself with vivacity and skill in the *Chroniques* as an investigator and a writer. He describes his travels and encounters; the bulk of Book Three is taken up by the story of his trip to Béarn and his information gathering both en route and at the court of Orthez. He often explains to the reader why he assembled the facts in a certain way, why he breaks off at a certain moment in order to go back to an earlier one. He acquits himself honorably in his bravura passages, and he is, in sum, a very agreeable writer to read.

Because they were so immensely successful, Froissart's *Chroniques* were continued. The Burgundian Enguerrand de Monstrelet carried them on for the period 1400–1444. His work was used in turn by Georges Chastellain, an official of the Burgundian court and a very famous writer in his day. Insofar as we can tell, his partially lost *Chroniques* covered the period from the assassination of Jean Sans-Peur in 1419 up to 1475. Chastellain, whom I have already mentioned as a poet, wrote an emphatic and declamatory prose, paying great attention to the rhythm and the periodicity of his sentences, traits characteristic of the *rhétoriqueurs*. Another *rhétoriqueur*, his disciple Jean Molinet, followed him as official historian of the Burgundian court. His work covered the years 1474–1506.

Philippe de Commynes's *Mémoires* were written from a completely different perspective. Born in 1447, he became a squire in the service of the count of Charolais, the future duke of Burgundy, Charles the Rash, in 1464 and was secretly "bought" by Louis XI on the occasion of the meeting between the king and the duke at Péronne in 1468. Continuing to carry out confidential missions for Duke Charles for several years, he finally abandoned him and fled to the French camp on the night of 7–8 August 1472. Favored by Louis XI, he at first played an important political role in the king's administration. He then fell into a sort of semi-disgrace that grew so bad during the regency of Anne de Beaujeu after the king's death (1483) that he even spent some time in prison. Despite his efforts, he never again played an important role in political affairs. He died in 1511.

Commynes's *Mémoires* were composed in large part in 1489–1490 and completed beween 1493 and 1498. They are, first, the work of an eyewitness seeking to uncover the basic causes of the events in which he took part. They are also, in a less obvious way, the personal defense of a man stained by treason. Third and finally, the lessons to be learned from the events Commynes relates, the portraits of sovereigns, and his observations concerning the characters of different peoples and the nature of different political systems, make them a sort of treatise on government for princes.

Not all the personal testimonies concerning this period exhibited as much ambition or detachment. But it is interesting that several appeared that did not have, in principle at least, any literary pretensions. At the end of the fourteenth century, Bishop Jean Le Fèvre, chancellor of Duke Louis I d'Anjou, kept a journal that has interested historians, especially for what he relates concerning the Great Schism. Written in an alert and effective style between 1405 and 1449, the *Journal d'un bourgeois de Paris* (*Journal of a Parisian Burgher*) offers a mine of information about the daily life—including the price of foodstuffs—and the opinions of a clerk who belonged to the Burgundian party and lived in the capital at the end of the Hundred Years' War.

As we will see, however, the true literary interest of all these works lies elsewhere, in the relation between the writing of history and of romance fiction that I mentioned in the discussion of Froissart. It also lies in the influence of contemporary daily life and political preoccupations—broadly understood—on various literary forms.

Political Thought

The new category of writers consisting of princely retainers and government officials did not manifest its interest in public affairs solely by telling the history of the times. These writers expressed this interest more directly by wrapping their political and moral reflections in literary forms.

This ambition is particularly evident among the counselors

of Charles V, and then those of the young Charles VI, at the court of France. It was one of these counselors who, in 1376, wrote the *Songe du verger* (*Dream of the Orchard*). Written in the conventional form of a dream, the *Songe* is a long prose dialogue between a clerk and a knight on the relations between the ecclesiastical and secular powers and, more specifically, on the pope's and the king's respective powers in France. It was written immediately after the truce of Bruges (1375) confirming Charles V's reconquest of France and dealt with a number of timely subjects: the questions of Brittany, of England, of the return of the pope to Rome, of the legal succession of women, and of the sovereignty of the king of France, the juridical foundation of Charles V's position in the negotiations at Bruges. Philippe de Mézières (1327–1405)—chancellor of the king of Cyprus, Pierre I de Lusignan, before becoming a close counselor to Charles V and the tutor of the dauphin, the future Charles VI—wrote for his pupil in 1389 the *Songe du vieil pélerin* (*Dream of the Old Pilgrim*), a work of "bonne policie" ("good advice"), whose teaching is both religious and political. Its goal was to prepare the soul for the conquest of the Kingdom of God, represented, for the former chancellor of Cyprus, by the trip to the Holy Land and the crusade. Guided by a narrator named Burning Desire, Queen Truth, accompanied by Justice, Peace, and Mercy, travels throughout the Orient and the Occident judging customs and institutions. At the end, she arrives in France, where she reviews society's various estates, up to the king. Reforms are proposed, and the last part of the work is a true treatise on government. In a less direct and more speculative way, and with the help of Aristotle, Nicole Oresme proposed a system of political ethics and reflected on the perverse consequences of the sophistication of currencies in his *Traictié des monnoies* (*Treatise on Monies*).

But the most illustrious work of this kind is the *Quadrilogue invectif* (*Vituperative Quadrilogue*) of Alain Chartier, whose influence on poetry has already been mentioned. Secretary to Charles VI, then to the dauphin, the future Charles VII, he composed the *Quadrilogue* in 1422 after the Treaty of Troyes (1420), during the kingdom's darkest hour. The work depicts a France clothed in mourning, weeping for her children. These latter, represented by the three estates, speak one after the other. The People lament their misery and despair, the Aristocracy its bitterness, and the Clergy formulates the conditions for a national recovery.

Others wrote about these questions with equal zeal but less competence. Christine de Pizan, for example, wrote a *Livre des faits et bonnes moeurs du roi Charles V* (*Book of the Deeds and Good Character of the King Charles V*) in 1404, a *Lettre à Isabeau de Bavière* (*Letter to Isabeau de Bavière*) in October 1405, a *Livre du corps de policie* (*Book of the Body of Policy*) between 1404 and 1407, a *Lamentation sur les maux de la guerre civile* (*Lament on the Evils of Civil War*) in 1410, and a *Livre de la paix* (*Book of Peace*), begun in 1412 and finished in 1414. Her last known work, written in 1429, is a *Ditié de Jeanne d'Arc* (*Poem of Joan of Arc*).

At this time, political preoccupations and themes rather curiously invaded a most unlikely literary form, the *pastorale* (pastoral poem). The *Dit de Franc-Gontier* (Dit *of Free Gontier*), a short poem written by Philippe de Vitry in the first half of the fourteenth century—of which Villon made much fun—had celebrated the rustic life, thus breaking with the *pastourelle*'s disdainful and mocking attitude towards it. This change in values characterized the passage from the *pastourelle* (a poem relating an encounter with a shepherdess) to the *pastorale* in which the shepherds' frolics become the mask for political propaganda. Froissart wrote several *pastourelles* in which the shepherds forget their loves and talk about current events. Written between 1422 and 1425, the *Pastoralet* relates the events of the reign of Charles VI under the cover of a *pastorale* and is a violently partisan Burgundian pamphlet.

The poetry of daily life defined in the preceding chapter naturally became a poetry of current events: Machaut depicts the calamaties of the day, Deschamps mourns the death of Du Guesclin. Imprisonment, a constant threat, became an important poetic theme. It appears, for example, in Machaut's *Confort d'ami* (*Friend's Comfort*), written for Charles de Navarre while he was the prisoner of Jean le Bon; in Froissart's *Dit du bleu chevalier* (*Poem of the Blue Knight*) and his *Prison amoureuse* (*Amorous Prison*), the allegorical description of the real captivity of Wenceslas de Brabant; and, in the following century, in the anonymous *Prisonnier desconforté* (*Forlorn Prisoner*), in Jean

Régnier's *Fortunes et adversités* (*Fortunes and Adversities*), and, of course, in the work of Charles d'Orléans.

Didacticism

This serious turn, this wisdom in letters, manifested itself out-side of the political domain in an abundance of didactic works. Some of these were works of edification and spirituality, of course, such as existed throughout the Middle Ages, but they took on a new aura when they were composed by someone like Jean Gerson (1363–1429), chancellor of the University of Paris, theologian, author of spiritual works in both Latin and French (*La Montagne de contemplation* [*The Mountain of Contemplation*], *La Mendicité spirituelle* [*Spiritual Mendicancy*], *La Médecine de l'âme* [*The Soul's Medicine*], *L'ABC des simples gens* [*The ABC of Common People*]), and one of the most respected people of his time. Others of these works had a moral aim, like those Chris-tine de Pizan wrote to comfort and defend women (*La Cité des Dames* [*The City of Ladies*], 1404–1405). Yet others were educa-tional works, like those written by the strange mystic and logi-cian Ramon Lull (c. 1232–1315) (*Doctrina pueril* [*On the Educa-tion of Children*], *Félix ou Le livre des merveilles* [*Felix or the Book of Marvels*], and the curious *Bildungsroman, Blanquerna*). The Angevin knight Geoffroy de La Tour Landry (c. 1330–c. 1405) wrote a *Livre pour l'enseignement de ses filles* (*Book for the Educa-tion of His Daughters*) that is simultaneously a book of memories and a collection of anecdotes and *exempla* from various sources. Around 1393, a rich, old Parisian burgher wrote the *Mesnagier de Paris* (*Housekeeper of Paris*)—a blend of religious instruction, advice concerning household management, and recipes—for his very young wife.

Many scientific works, or works setting forth practical knowl-edge, were written, even in French: astronomical, astrological, and medical treatises, books on the art of hunting, (that of Froissart's host, Gaston Phébus, is the most famous), or the art of war. Some of the treatises on warfare aim at nothing more than an exposition of evolving military techniques (*Art d'archerie* [*Art of Archery*], *Art d'artillerie* [*Art of Artillery*]) or the codifica-tion of the procedures for jousts and tournaments (like Geoffroy de Charny's *Demandes pour les joutes, les tournois et la guerre* [*Challenges for Jousts, Tournaments and War*], or René d'Anjou's

Livre des tournois [*Book of Tournaments*]), but others reflected on the rules of war and the relations between force and rights. In his *Livre de chevalerie* (*Book of Chivalry*), for example, Geoffroy de Charny—killed at the battle of Poitiers in 1356 while carrying the Oriflamme, the royal banner of France—tried only to defend the rules of chivalry, threatened by the techniques of modern warfare, without considering the consequences of the war for civilians. Honoré Bovet, however, prior of Salon, had an altogether different goal in his *Arbre des batailles* (*Tree of Battles*). Written in the last years of the fourteenth century, this was a true legal treatise on the conduct of war, concerned with the protection of non-combattants and their property (churchmen, students, merchants, and, above all, peasants), which the ongoing exactions of military forces made especially timely. The success of this work was immense—even if it had no practical effect whatsoever. It was invoked in fifteenth-century treatises the way one would today invoke the Geneva Conventions; and Christine de Pizan pillaged it, as well as a French translation of Vegetius's *Rei militaris instituta* or *Epitoma rei militaris* (*Military Precepts* or *Military Epitome*) for her *Livre des faits d'armes et de chevalerie* (*Book of Deeds of Arms and Chivalry*, 1410). The *Jouvencel* (*Young Man*, 1461–1466) of Jean de Bueil, admiral of France, finally, is a sort of treatise on military education in the form of the semi-autobiographical story of a poor young man at the end of the Hundred Years' War.

From Clerk to Humanist
Alongside this didactic effort, of which the few examples cited above can give only a very feeble idea, a more profound mutation was taking place affecting the very conception of intellectual life and knowledge. A new spirit began to be felt from Italy in the fourteenth century, where Petrarch sought to restore to antiquity its true character, hidden behind its scholastic formalization. Classical authors were translated in France as well: Livy, for example, by Pierre Bersuire in the reign of Jean le Bon (1350–1364), and Aristotle by Nicole Oresme (c. 1320–1382) at the request of Charles V. Grand Master of the Collège de Navarre, later the king's secretary, and finally bishop of Lisieux, Oresme left an *oeuvre* of considerable importance, in both Latin and French. He was an excellent mathematician and possessed

a positive turn of mind that led him, for example, to denounce the dangers of occultism in the *Traictié de la Divination* (*Treatise on Divination*). Several years later, a circle of lively minds, participants in the "Quarrel of the Rose," formed around the Collège de Navarre, including Nicolas de Clamanges, Gontier and Pierre Col, and Jean de Montreuil. They were in touch with the intellectual life of Italy, corresponded with the chancellor of Florence, Coluccio Salutati, and sought to rediscover the purity of classical Latin and a classical epistolary elegance, but did not disdain to write in French or lose interest in the difficulties of their times. In the first years of the fifteenth century, Jean de Montreuil defended the rights of the French king against the pretentions of the English in satires composed in both Latin and French. The influence of these pre-humanists was not immediately decisive. It was not until the years 1450–1470 that Guillaume Fichet, who installed the first printing press at the University of Paris, called for the abandonment of scholastic exercises and a return to classical eloquence. But it is clear in retrospect that the great thirteenth-century synthesis of knowledge was tottering already at the very beginning of the fifteenth century and a new type of intellectual was ready to appear, one who was not a clerk—that indissociable combination of churchman and scholar—but was both more critical and more solitary.

11   *The Forms of Representation*

The Representation of a World

The dying Middle Ages' tendency to become intoxicated with its own image has often been judged harshly. A world apparently ignorant or unmindful of its own decline seems to have contemplated itself smugly in a series of chivalric or princely spectacles. Few periods, it is true, have participated so willingly in their own theatrical representation. Every royal entry, whose smallest details were related in the chronicles, combined several spectacles: the princely cortege in its power and glory; the living tableaux, dramatic fragments that came to life as they passed and revealed the meaning of the occasion through the correspondences of allegory; and the emblematic representations of plenty (banquets to which everyone was invited, fountains running with wine, and so on). Consecration, coronation, surrender, diplomatic reception or conference, trial, execution: everything served—as did plays themselves—as an occasion for theatrical self-representation. Even the physical and moral misery of the human condition was exhibited uninhibitedly in the performances of the *Danse macabré* (Dance of Death) and its literary equivalents.

Chivalric society liked especially to contemplate itself in the mirror of literature and to dress itself up like the models it found in romances. It loved to re-enact the adventures of romance heroes, so there were many feasts and tournaments with Arthurian themes. Inspired by an episode of *Alixandre l'Orphelin* (*Alexander the Orphan*), for example, Jean de Luxembourg defended the "Pas de la Belle Pélerine" (the *Pas*, or Passage of Arms, of the Beautiful Pilgrim) against any adversary who bore the arms of Lancelot or Palamède. When King René d'Anjou organized an *emprise et pas* (contest and passage of arms) near Chinon, he borrowed its name, the "Joyeuse Garde," from the castle of the prose *Lancelot*. For an entire year, from fall 1449 to fall 1450, Jacques de Lalaing defended a "Fontaine de Pleurs" ("Spring of Tears") in Burgundy against all comers for a "Dame de Pleurs" ("Lady of Tears"). A book in the form of a romance was written about the exploits of this very real person (the *Livre des faits de Jacques Lalaing* [*Book of Jacques Lalaing's Deeds*]), and there was also a *Livre des faits du maréchal de Boucicaut* (*Book of the Deeds of the Marshal de Boucicaut*). The coats of arms of the knights of the Round Table were likewise established in great detail at this time. Chivalric society sought to bring the romance past to life and to endow life with the colors of a romance.

The Mirror of Romance

The romance world was more than ever a past world. The values and imagination of the current day were projected into the past along with the action of the romances. It might at first seem that there was nothing new in this—the first romances and the *chansons de geste* had done the same—but at the end of the Middle Ages, the antiquity of the events was reinforced by that of literature itself. Arthur, Charlemagne, Alexander had not only lived a long time ago, they had also been spoken and written about for a long time. At the beginning of the romance *Ysaïe le Triste* (*Sad Ysaïe*), whose protagonists are the son and grandson of Tristan and Isolde, the author emphasizes the longevity of the Arthurian world by telling us that, at the time his story begins, Arthur is very old and some of the knights of the Round Table have already died. Not only had all these characters lived long, long ago, their literary life was also already very long, so long that they had become old. And they had not been living this life in a cultural Other World, in classical antiquity or some uncertain folkloric or pseudo-historical tradition, as they had when they were taken up in the first French romances; they had been living it in the familiar world of the romances themselves, in the chronologically, culturally, and linguistically immediate predecessors and models of the late medieval romances.

For the first time, French literature enjoyed the perspectives opened up for it by its own past. It discovered that fashions and language grow old. It discovered that the French spoken two or three centuries before, that of the twelfth or thirteenth century, was Old French, different from the modern language and almost incomprehensible.

This discovery is reflected in the romance genre's two most striking traits at the end of the Middle Ages: the relative rareness, on the one hand, of entirely new works—although some new works were very successful, like *Mélusine*, whose two versions, one in prose by Jean d'Arras and one in verse by Coudrette, date to the end of the fourteenth century—and the abundance, on the other hand, of *mises en prose*. These *mises en prose* ([works] put in prose), as their name suggests, were prose adaptations of verse romances or *chansons de geste* of the twelfth or thirteenth century. Both romances and *chansons de geste* could be adapted in this way because the general use of prose made the old distinction between these narrative genres unimportant, founded in large part as it was on opposing poetic forms, themselves linked to different modes of reception. The dissolution of the different literary genres and the various modes of reception reduced them to a single form—prose narrative divided into chapters—and created a situation in which the audience's expectations were the same regardless of whether the story came from a *chanson de geste*, an Arthurian romance, a romance of antiquity, or a saint's life. The distinct visions of the world that had belonged to these genres lost their specificity for the reader and melted together in a kind of ideological syncretism common to all narrative literature. Certain romances of a somewhat hybrid nature, which had been largely unsuccessful in their original verse form, were thus widely read in their later prose adaptations: *Bérinus*, for example, or *Belle Hélène de Constantinople* (*Beautiful Helen of Constantinople*), or, under slightly different conditions, *Apollonius de Tyr* (*Apollonius of Tyr*). Everything was grist for prose's mill. No matter how faithful each individual prose adaptation was to its original, the literary corpus constituted by the adaptations had its own, new tone and values.

Historiography became the model for romance writing and the romance genre regained the aura of historicity it had had in its beginnings. In the fifteenth century, the Burgundian David Aubert compiled the whole of the epic tradition and entitled his enormous work the *Chroniques et conquestes de Charlemagne* (*Chronicles and Conquests of Charlemagne*). Narratives of antiqui-

ty and the crusades were reforged and given a stronger historical coloring, even when the sources of the new works were
entirely romance or epic, even when the marvelous played a
major role in their plots. At the beginning of the fourteenth-
century *Baudouin de Flandres* (*Baldwin of Flanders*), a count of
Flanders marries a devil who has possessed the dead body of an
Oriental princess. This motif, well known in Indian and Oriental literature, appears again a little later in *Richard sans peur*
(*Fearless Richard*), a sequel to *Robert le Diable* (*Robert the Devil*),
which, rather than concentrating on the adventures of a hero,
chronicles the careers of several characters during the reigns of
Philippe II Augustus (1179–1223), Saint Louis (1226–1270)
and Philippe III le Hardi (1270–1285). It rewrites the history of
the Battle of Bouvines and the Seventh Crusade and gives
fantastic destinies to historical figures like Ferrant de Flandres
or Jean Tristan, count of Nevers. In reality, this third son of
Saint Louis was born at Damietta in 1250 and died of dysen-
tery before the walls of Tunis in 1270. In the romance, he
becomes the king's oldest son and is provided with a singularly
animated life. The tale ends, not with a narrative dénouement,
but with the death of Philippe III and the accession of Philippe
IV le Bel.

Princely patronage favored genealogical romances written on
command for the glory of a family, describing its origins—both
historical and mythical—and its illustrious members. Such
romances include the *Histoire des seigneurs de Gavre* (*History of
the Lords of Gavre*), the two versions of *Mélusine*, written at the
request of relatives of the Lusignan family, and *Fouke le Fitz
Warin* (*Fulk the Son of Warin*) and *Guy de Warwik* (*Guy of
Warwick*), which continued the Anglo-Norman tradition of the
family romance. The romances written at the court of Burgundy—the *Roman du comte d'Artois* (*Romance of the Count of Artois*), for example, or Raoul Le Fèvre's *Histoire de Jason et de
Médée* (*History of Jason and Medea*), the latter clearly linked to
the creation of the Order of the Golden Fleece in 1430—were
only too happy to take advantage of their historical aura in
order to flatter the duke by allusions or implicit parallels. The
prose adaptations of even the most "classical" and least historical romances of the preceding period tried to move them in the
direction of history. The adaptors added chronological referenc-

es, allusions to real events and people, and, in prologues and epilogues, a great many details concerning dynastic and family history. One finds these traits, for example, in the prose adaptations of Chrétien de Troyes's *Erec et Enide* (*Erec and Enide*) and *Cligès*, of Adenet le Roi's *Cléomadés*, of Jakemes's *Roman du Châtelain de Coucy et de la Dame de Fayel* (*Romance of the Chatelain of Coucy and the Lady of Fayel*), and in many others.

Many romances also manifested the educational or pedagogical concerns animating works that claimed to be true accounts, like the *Livre des faits de Jacques Lalaing* and the *Livre des faits du maréchal de Boucicaut*. These concerns are to be found in "Breton" romances like *Ysaïe le Triste* or *Perceforest* as well as in romances like Antoine de la Sale's *Jehan de Saintré* that are set in a more recent past and are similar, in certain respects, to the *Livre de Jacques Lalaing*.

Verse romances did not suddenly disappear, however. Many were still written in the fourteenth century. But the hegemony of prose, considered more and more to be the natural form of romance narration, gave verse a particular value even as it forced it to retreat. Writing in verse could be simply nostalgic—it clearly was for Froissart, who wrote a long Arthurian romance, *Méliador*, in verse when none had been written since Gerard d'Amiens's *Escanor* a century earlier—or it could be the result of the kind of conservatism one finds in semi-popular or artistically unsophisticated works like *Eledus et Serena* (*Eledus and Serena*) or *Brun de la Montagne* (*Brun of the Mountain*).

Verse romances could also be given the affective, subjective coloring that was beginning to characterize verse as such and that led, as we have seen, to a new concept of poetry. These romances thus often tended to treat amorous adventures in allegorical terms, even if this allegorization remained discreet and semi-implicit, as in the *Roman de la Dame à la Licorne et du Beau Chevalier au Lion* (*Romance of the Lady with the Unicorn and the Handsome Knight with the Lion*). Between this work, which remains a true romance, and the *dits* describing an allegorical dream or telling the tale of an amorous adventure, which are not romances despite their narrative character, there are a number of intermediate poems or poems mixing verse and prose that are difficult to classify and which create a continuity between the verse romance and the *dit*. These poems include amorous *dits* influenced by the *Roman de la Rose* (like Jean Bras-de-Fer de Dammartin-en-Goële's *Pamphile et Galatée* [*Pamphile and Galatée*], which introduces passages inspired directly by Jean de Meun into a translation of its Latin model), and romances of the self, products of a cross between allegorical and "Breton" romances (like Marquis Thomas III de Saluces's *Chevalier errant* [*Wandering Knight*] or, later, King René I d'Anjou's *Livre du cuer d'Amours espris* [*Book of the Heart Inflamed with Love*]). The *Chevalier errant* borrows whole passages from the *Roman de la Rose*, but the conception of the romance is quite original; it is not simply the work of a plagiarist. The *Livre du cuer d'Amours espris*, whose narration conforms more to the romance model, makes no effort to hide that it was inspired by the *Roman de la Rose* and Arthurian romances. The work of princely dilettantes, the work of readers, these romances synthesized the subjective elements of narrative that seduced and nourished the imaginations of their time.

The birth of humanism seems to have given a new value to verse in the very last years of the fifteenth century. For Octovien de Saint-Gelais, at least, a verse translation like his *Enéide ou Eurialus et Lucrèce* (*Aeneid or Eurialus and Lucretia*) offered clear evidence of its author's delicate, sophisticated sensibility—even if the verses were execrable.

As the verse romance became increasingly marginal at the end of the Middle Ages, the narrative form that blossomed and whose development was the most fertile was the *nouvelle* (novella). Various collections of *nouvelles* appeared along the road leading from Boccaccio's *Decameron* to Marguerite de Navarre's *Heptaméron*, such as, to name only one, the *Cent nouvelles nouvelles* (*One Hundred New Novellas*) from the middle of the fifteenth century. The *nouvelle* quickly came under the influence of Italian literature just as other genres would somewhat later. From the *fabliau* tradition that it continued, the *nouvelle* inherited its deliberately provocative tone, and to this it joined a polemical reflection on love and the place of women in society. This reflection was linked to the quarrel about feminism, as the misogyny of the *Quinze joies du mariage* (*Fifteen Joys of Marriage*) testifies, and also continued the courtly debates of amorous casuistry like those found in Martial d'Auvergne's *Arrêts d'Amour* (*Decrees of Love*), where the exposition of each "case" is the pretext for an anecdote. Unlike the romance, turned entirely towards the past, the *nouvelle* was set in the present. It put its values to the test, whereas the romance celebrated and justified its values by projecting them into the past. The *nouvelle* was critical, the romance emphatic. The relation between the romance and the *nouvelle* is clearly visible in Antoine de La Sale's *Jehan de Saintré*, a romance leaning towards the *nouvelle*. The duplicity of the lady of Belles Cousines, the triumphant vulgarity of her lover the abbot, the humiliation of Jehan de Saintré, the cruelty of his revenge: all this flies in the face of the elegant perfection traditionally attributed to courtly loves and the chivalric universe, the appearance of which the romance retains. As soon as the romance past was no longer there to embellish them, contemporary morals appeared as base as they truly were. It is because they refused the illusion of the past that the fifteenth-century authors of *nouvelles* seem to us to have been moralists.

The modern novel is thus the child of the *nouvelle*. The medieval romance, the romance of chivalry, had a more marginal, limited destiny. Many copies of the late-medieval romances were printed from the end of the fifteenth century on— and nourished the dreams of Don Quixote. But little by little they became popular literature, and survived—some of them up until the nineteenth century—as a sort of early dime novel. It was in this form—eclipsed but widely read—that they waited patiently for the late eighteenth century to rediscover the Middle Ages.

Theater

The mirror of romance was a metaphoric mode of representation. But the late Middle Ages was the period of all kinds of representations and theatrical self-representations. It was the period of theater's, and above all of religious theater's, great development. The "miracles par personages" ("miracles performed by characters"), or theatrical representations of miracle stories, of which Jean Bodel's *Jeu de saint Nicolas* (*Play of Saint Nicholas*) and Rutebeuf's *Miracle de Théophile* (*Miracle of Théophile*) were the first representatives, multiplied and were often composed at the request of confraternities who wished to honor their patron saint. The miracles of the saints or the *Miracles de*

Notre Dame (*Miracles of Our Lady*)—these latter transposing into
theatrical form old narrative collections of which the best
known was that of Gautier de Coincy (c. 1177–1236)—each
dealt with a single miracle performed by the saint or the Virgin
from his or her celestial abode. Mystery plays, on the other
hand, told the story of a saint's entire life or of an entire book
or episode of the Bible. Their performance, in combination with
that of a morality play (a didactic play on a religious, moral, or
political subject with allegorical characters) or a farce, lasted an
entire day. Sometimes, in the case of the great mystery plays of
the Passion or of the Acts of the Apostles, these performances
lasted for several days. They were organized at great expense by
towns, and their staging required elaborate machinery and
special effects, especially the staging of tortures and punish-
ments. The entire population helped to prepare the spectacle
and attended its performance, surrounding the circular "stage"
which might take up an entire town square.[1] In the fifteenth
century, mystery plays representing the Passion—like that of
Eustache Mercadé (1420) or the admirable one by Arnoul
Gréban (1452) which was reworked and amplified by Jean
Michel in 1486—might run to tens of thousands of lines (Jean
Michel's has almost 35,000). Far from limiting themselves to
the Passion, they began with the creation of humankind and
traced the expectation of the Savior and God's promise
throughout the entire Old Testament, providing a vast meditation on the history of salvation, the relations between God and
humankind, and the economy of redemption. They were not
afraid to introduce apocryphal elements, like the legend that
Judas was both incestuous and a parricide, and to blend in
touching or comic scenes from everyday life, even burlesques
involving demons. Arnoul et Simon Gréban's long *Mystère des
actes des Apôtres* (*Mystery of the Acts of the Apostles*, 62,000 lines)
continued Arnoul's *Passion* by representing the history of na-
scent Christianity in the heart of the Roman world.

Some mystery plays dealt with secular subjects, like the
Mystère du siège d'Orléans (*Mystery of the Siege of Orléans*, 1453),

---

[1] See H. Rey-Flaud, *Le Cercle magique: Essai sur le théâtre en rond à la fin du
moyen âge* (Paris: Gallimard, 1973).

roughly contemporary with the reinstatement of Joan of Arc, or Jacques Milet's *Mystère de la destruction de Troie la Grant* (*Mystery of the Destruction of Great Troy*, 1452). Twenty-seven thousand lines long and divided into four days, Milet's *Mystère* was dedicated to Charles VII and was the first play to portray the classical world and exploit the myth of the Trojan origin of the Franks. There likewise existed edifying miracle plays like *Griseldis* that were not, strictly speaking, religious.

Comic theater was not so ambitious and did not go to such lengths. It took the form of short pieces (300 to 500 lines) and was divided into two principal genres, the *sottie*, or fools' play, and the farce. Often linked to the activities of joyous confraternities like the "Enfants sans souci" (Heedless Children) of Paris or the "Cornards" (Horners) of Rouen, the *sottie* developed in urban intellectual milieux, especially in the world of the schools around such groups as the "Clercs de la Basoche" (Clerks of the Basoche, a brotherhood of clerks and lawyers) of Paris. Recognizable by their peculiar outfits, the fools elected a "Prince des Sots" (Prince of Fools) and a "Mère Sotte" (Mother Fool). Composed of paradoxes and nonsense, their discourse was assumed to harbor more truth (albeit in a concealed form) than the everyday discourses of common sense. The *sotties*, especially those produced in the milieux of the Basoche, parodied the procedures of a real trial in which the accused were named "Chacun" (Everyone) or "les Gens" (the People). After the verdict had been delivered, the judge ordered the fools to reform the realm (as in, for example, the *Sottie des Sots triomphants qui trompent Chacun* [Sottie *of the Triumphant Fools Who Fool Everyone*], or the *Sottie pour le cry de la Basoche* [Sottie *for the Proclamation of the Basoche*]). Other *sotties* portrayed social types belonging, generally, to supposedly wretched or disgraceful categories. The underlying satire was not unlike that animating the reviews of the estates of the world in the preceding period, even though the tone was altogether different and the coloring was far more political, as one sees, for example, in André de La Vigne's *Sottie à VII personnages* (Sottie *for Seven Characters*, 1507). Beneath a seemingly total freedom, the verbal fantasy, the puns, the non sequiturs, and the constant play on *agnominatio* (repetition of a word with a different meaning or spelling) were profoundly and closely related to the virtuosity of the *grands rhétoriqueurs*.

The farce systematically exploited the commonplaces of sudden reversals that transform the deceiver into the deceived and the effects to be drawn from them. Closely linked to the spirit of the *fabliau*, the farce frequently portrays love triangles discovered by the *badin*, a naive character who, taking everything literally, unintentionally reveals the truth and ridicules conventions. The lines of the farce are sometimes divided into stanzas in order to permit the introduction of comic verses and snatches of comic songs into the dialogue. Some of them play out the literal meaning of a proverb, like the *Farce des éveilleurs du chat qui dort* (*The Farce of the Wakers of the Sleeping Cat*) and the *Farce des femmes qui font accroire à leurs marys de vecies que ce sont lanternes* (*The Farce of the Wives Who Make Their Husbands Think that Bladders Are Lanterns*). The best known, and the most elaborate, is the *Farce de maître Pierre Pathelin* (*Farce of Master Pierre Pathelin*), perhaps written between 1461 and 1469.

All these dramatic forms belong as much to the sixteenth century as to the late Middle Ages, even though the mystery plays, whose orthodoxy was sometimes suspect, did not survive the Reformation and were banned, in Paris at least, in 1548. There was thus no clear rupture, no interruption in theatrical forms at the end of the fifteenth century—just as there was not in other literary forms. The *grands rhétoriqueurs* were as much poets of the sixteenth century as they were of the fifteenth, "medieval" lyric forms were prominent and commonly practiced for a long time, and the romances of chivalry made the fortune of many a printer. When Pierre Sala from Lyon (who died around 1530), the author of a *Tristan et Iseut* (*Tristan and Isolde*), presented François I with his "latest" work, it was an adaptation of Chrétien de Troyes's *Chevalier au lion* (*Knight with the Lion*). Montaigne cited Froissart. The Middle Ages were not discovered by the Romantics. They have never ceased to nourish French literature.

Conclusion

At the end of the last chapter I stressed that medieval literature survived well beyond the end of the Middle Ages. It would be easy to develop this theme, for example, by enumerating the names of those who read, loved and publicized it, well or badly, during periods when it is usually considered to have been forgotten or despised. I could thus cite pell-mell Jean de Notre-Dame, Claude Fauchet, Voiture, Du Cange. It would be easy to point out that the hagiographical and romance narratives of the Middle Ages were at the heart of the success of the "Bibliothèque bleue" ("Blue Library," an early seventeenth-century series of popular books, sold door-to-door) and, later, of the *Bibliothèque universelle des romans* (*Universal Library of Novels*, a literary periodical containing condensed versions of popular stories and novels, published between 1775 and 1789). It would be easy to invoke the eighteenth-century novelists, Baculard d'Arnaud or Madame de Genlis, who set the action of their novels in the Middle Ages even before the Romantics made it fashionable to do so, even before Chateaubriand's *Génie du Christianisme* (*The Genius of Christianity*) opposed the monarchistic and Christian Middle Ages to the revolutionary world inspired by classical antiquity.

It would thus be easy to demonstrate the survival of medieval literature, too easy in fact. A few examples do not permit us to dispute the general rule. For it is indeed true, in general, that the Middle Ages and medieval literature were rediscovered in the nineteenth century thanks to the influence of the Romantics, who sought to define a nation's spirit by digging into the roots of its traditional culture and going back to its past. Whence the long-standing association between studies of folklore and medieval studies. Whence also the illusions and the ambiguities that grew up around the idea of popular poetry, illusions which positivistic philology, established on a scientific model at the end of the nineteenth century, sought to dissipate, only to replace them, sometimes, with other errors. It is indeed true, in general, that French literature refused its medieval heritage for several centuries and that, when it finally accepted it, its new enthusiasm was based partly on a misunderstanding.

What, then, made medieval literature so different from that of succeeding centuries? Or, more precisely, how was the medieval idea of literature different from that of later periods? In trying to give a brief answer to such a question, I am sure to answer it badly. If required to do so, however, I would suggest that unlike classical and modern literature, medieval literature had hardly any use for the notion of inspiration and none whatsoever for that of genius. No *furor* (poetic madness), no *numen* (divine inspiration), no Mount Parnassos (sacred to Apollo, home of the Muses) or Apollo (god of poetry), no Muses (goddesses of arts and sciences), driven out—and for a long time—by Boethius' Philosophy because they were useless and unable to console the prisoner. By returning to all this, the poets of the Pléiade (a Renaissance poetic movement) were indeed doing something new, and Boileau (a seventeenth-century poet and critic) followed them on this point, conceding that poetry requires more than simply work. No appeal either to overflowing feelings as the source of poetic creation in the Romantic manner. A consequence of the tendency, then new, to see love as the principal subject of literature, the medieval association between amorous passion and poetic creation, in which Romanticism thought it recognized itself, did indeed make the poem a product of feelings, but in an almost abstract application of general rules. For the rest, it was only a question of competence, culture, and work. Authors boasted only of knowing their subject, mastering their sources, and writing with care. What is needed to compose a poem? Froissart answers at the beginning of the *Joli buisson de jeunesse* (*Pretty Thicket of Youth*):

> . . . sens et memore,
> Encre, papier et escriptore,
> Kanivet et penne taillie,
> Et volonté appareillie.

(. . . understanding and memory, ink, paper, and writing desk, knife and sharpened quill, and a ready will.)

For the last two hundred years, however, medieval literature has constantly held a certain fascination for scholars and readers. It has thus not been taken to task too heavily for this peculiar characteristic, especially because the confusion between amorous and poetic inspiration allowed it to be ignored for a long time. When the small importance attached to inspiration in medieval literature was finally recognized a few decades ago, attempts to theorize and formalize literary activity were at their height. Medieval authors were thus congratulated for their modernity. This modernity, of course, did not exist, and many interpretations which were proposed then seem today to be as obsolete as those of a hundred years ago.

Medieval literature cannot be approached through the conventional distinctions of other periods, including our own, but neither is it as off-putting and glacial as has sometimes been suggested and as one might at first think. The effusion and portrayal of the self, like the depth of mystery and the seduction of narrative, were not strangers to it; in fact, far from it. But it established its own equilibrium between feelings and the intellect, between imagination and the faithful representation of the world, between imitation and renewal. It is not futile to attempt to understand and appreciate this literature. First and foremost, because it is pleasurable, but also because the discovery of a world which was simultaneously so near and so far from our own invites us to take a new look at ourselves.

Select Bibliography

Bibliographies, Manuals, Histories

Badel, P. Y. *Introduction à la vie littéraire du Moyen Age*. 2d ed. Paris: Bordas, 1984.

Baumgartner, E. *Histoire de la littérature française: Moyen Age (1050–1486)*. Paris: Bordas, 1987.

Beaumarchais, J.-P. de, D. Couty, A. Rey, eds. *Dictionnaire des littératures de langue française*. 3 vols. Paris: Bordas, 1984.

Bossuat, R. *Manuel bibliographique de la littérature française du Moyen Age*. Paris: d'Argences, 1951. *Supplément (1949–53)*, with J. Monfrin. Paris: d'Argences, 1955. *Second supplément (1954–60)*. Paris: d'Argences, 1961. *Troisième supplément (1960–80)*, by F. Vielliard and J. Monfrin. 2 vols. Paris: Editions du CNRS, 1986–91.

Fox, J. H. *The Middle Ages*. A Literary History of France, vol. 1. New York: Barnes & Noble, 1974.

Grente, G., et al., eds. *Dictionnaire des lettres françaises*. Vol. 1, *Le Moyen Age*, ed. R. Bossuat, L. Pichard, G. Raynaud de Lage. Paris: Fayard, 1964.

Grundriss der romanischen Literaturen des Mittelalters. Heidelberg: Carl Winter Verlag. Vol. 1, *Généralités*, ed. M. Delbouille. 1972. Vol. 4, *Le Roman jusqu'à la fin du XIIIe siècle*, ed. J. Frappier and R. Grimm. 2 vols. 1978–84. Vol. 6, *La Littérature didactique, allégorique et satirique*, ed. H. R. Jauss. 2 vols. 1968–70. Vol. 8, *La Littérature française aux XIVe et XVe siècles*, ed. D. Poirion. 1 vol. to date. 1988.

Hollier, D., ed. *A New History of French Literature*. Cambridge, Mass.: Harvard Univ. Press, 1989.

Lacy, N. J., ed. *The New Arthurian Encyclopedia*. New York: Garland, 1991.

Lacy, N. J., and G. Ashe. *The Arthurian Handbook*. New York: Garland, 1988.

Poirion, D., ed. *Précis de littérature française du Moyen Age*. Paris: Presses Universitaires de France, 1983.

Reid, J. M. H., ed. *The Concise Oxford Dictionary of French Literature*. Oxford: Clarendon, 1976.

Strayer, J., ed. *Dictionary of the Middle Ages*. 12 vols. New York: Scribner's, 1982–89.

Taylor, R. A. *La Littérature occitane du Moyen Age. Bibliographie sélective et critique.* Toronto: Univ. of Toronto Press, 1977.

Dictionaries, Grammars, Textual Editing

Bennett, P. E., and G. A. Runnalls. *The Editor and the Text.* Edinburgh: Edinburgh Univ. Press, 1990.

Einhorn, E. *Old French: A Concise Handbook.* Cambridge: Cambridge Univ. Press, 1974.

Foulet, A., and M. B. Speer. *On Editing Old French Texts.* Lawrence: Regents Press of Kansas, 1979.

Fox, J., and R. Wood. *A Concise History of the French Language (Phonology and Morphology).* Oxford: Blackwell, 1968.

Godefroy, F. *Dictionnaire de l'ancienne langue française et de tous ses dialectes du IXe au XVe siècle.* 10 vols. Paris: F. Vieweg (vols. 1–5) and E. Bouillon (vols. 6–10), 1880–1902.

———. *Lexique de l'ancien français.* Paris: H. Welter, 1901; rpt. Paris: Champion, 1965.

Greimas, A. J. *Dictionnaire de l'ancien français jusqu'au milieu du XIVe siècle.* Paris: Larousse, 1968.

Kibler, W. *An Introduction to Old French.* New York: Modern Language Assoc. of America, 1984.

Rohlfs, G. *From Vulgar Latin to Old French: An Introduction to the Study of the Old French Language.* Trans. V. Almazen and L. McCarthy. Detroit: Wayne State Univ. Press, 1970.

Tobler, A., and E. Lommatzsch. *Altfranzösisches Wörterbuch.* Berlin: Weidmann, 1915–.

Critical Works

Arden, H. *Fools' Plays: A Study of Satire in the Sottie.* Cambridge: Cambridge Univ. Press, 1980.

Badel, P. Y. *Le Roman de la Rose au XIVe siècle: Etude de la réception de l'oeuvre.* Geneva: Droz, 1980.

Baswell, C., and W. Sharpe, eds. *The Passing of Arthur: New Essays in the Arthurian Tradition.* New York: Garland, 1988.

Baumgartner, E. *Tristan et Iseut.* Paris: Presses Universitaires de France, 1987.

Bédier, J. *Les Fabliaux.* Paris: Champion, 1893.

———. *Les Légendes épiques.* 4 vols. Paris: Champion, 1908–13.

Benton, J. F. *Culture, Power and Personality in Medieval France.* Ed. T. N. Bisson. London: Hambledon Press, 1991.

Berkvam, D. D. *Enfance et maternité dans la littérature française des XIIe et XIIIe siècles.* Paris: Champion, 1981.

Bezzola, R. R. *Les Origines et la formation de la littérature courtoise en Occident (500–1200).* 5 vols. Paris: Champion, 1944–67.

Blakeslee, M. *Love's Masks: Identity, Intertextuality, and Meaning in the Old French Tristan Poems*. Cambridge: D. S. Brewer; Wolfboro, N.H.: Boydell & Brewer, 1989.

Bloch, R. H. *Etymologies and Genealogies: A Literary Anthropology of the French Middle Ages*. Chicago: Univ. of Chicago Press, 1983.

———. *Medieval French Literature and Law*. Berkeley: Univ. of California Press, 1977.

———. *The Scandal of the Fabliaux*. Chicago: Univ. of Chicago Press, 1986.

Bogin, M. *The Women Troubadours*. New York: Norton, 1976.

Bossuat, R. *Le Roman de Renart*. Paris: Hatier, 1967.

Boutet, D. *Les Fabliaux*. Paris: Presses Universitaires de France, 1985.

Boutet, D., and A. Strubel. *Littérature, politique et société dans la France du moyen âge*. Paris: Presses Universitaires de France, 1979.

Brown, C. *The Shaping of History and Poetry in Late Medieval France: Propaganda and Artistic Expression in the Works of the Rhétoriqueurs*. Birmingham: Summa, 1985.

Brownlee, K. *Poetic Identity in Guillaume de Machaut*. Madison: Univ. of Wisconsin Press, 1984.

Bruckner, M. *Narrative Invention in Twelfth-Century French Romance: The Convention of Hospitality (1160–1200)*. Lexington, Ky.: French Forum, 1980.

Calin, W. *The Epic Quest: Studies in Four Old French Chansons de Geste*. Baltimore: Johns Hopkins Univ. Press, 1966.

———. *A Muse for Heroes: Nine Centuries of the Epic in France*. Toronto: Univ. of Toronto Press, 1983.

———. *The Old French Epic of Revolt: "Raoul de Cambrai," "Renaud de Montauban," "Gormond et Isembard"*. Geneva: Droz, 1962.

Cerquiglini, J. *"Un engin si soutil": Guillaume de Machaut et l'écriture au XIVe siècle*. Paris: Champion, 1985.

Chance, J., ed. *The Mythographic Art: Classical Fable and the Rise of the Vernacular in Early France and England*. Gainesville: Univ. of Florida Press, 1990.

Cholakian, R. *The Troubadour Lyric: A Psychocritical Reading*. New York: St. Martin's, 1990.

Colby, A. *The Portrait in Twelfth-Century French Literature: An Example of the Stylistic Originality of Chrétien de Troyes*. Geneva: Droz, 1965.

Cook, T. *The Old French and Chaucerian Fabliaux: A Study of Their Comic Climax*. Columbia: Univ. of Missouri Press, 1978.

Cook, T., and B. Honeycutt, eds. *The Humor of the Fabliaux: A Collection of Critical Essays*. Columbia: Univ. of Missouri Press, 1974.

Curtius, E. R. *European Literature and the Latin Middle Ages*. Trans. Willard R. Trask. Princeton: Princeton Univ. Press, 1953.

Dane, J. *Res/Verba: A Study in Medieval French Drama*. Leiden: Brill, 1985.

Daniel, N. *Heroes and Saracens: An Interpretation of the Chansons de Geste.* Edinburgh: Edinburgh Univ. Press, 1981.

Davenson, H. (H. I. Marrou). *Les Troubadours.* Paris: Le Seuil, 1961.

Dragonetti, R. *Le Mirage des sources: L'Art du faux dans le roman médiéval.* Paris: Le Seuil, 1987.

———. *La Technique poétique des trouvères dans la chanson courtoise: Contribution à l'étude de la rhétorique médiévale.* Bruges: De Tempel, 1960.

Duby, G. *The Chivalrous Society.* Trans. C. Postan. Berkeley: Univ. of California Press, 1980.

Dufournet, J. *La Destruction des mythes dans les Mémoires de Philippe de Commynes.* Geneva: Droz, 1966.

———. *Les Ecrivains de la IVe croisade: Villehardouin et Clari.* 2 vols. Paris: SEDES, 1973.

Duggan, J. *The Song of Roland: Formulaic Style and Poetic Craft.* Berkeley: Univ. of California Press, 1973.

Faral, E. *Les Jongleurs en France au Moyen Age.* Paris: Champion, 1910.

———. *La Légende arthurienne.* 3 vols. Paris: Champion, 1929.

Frank, G. *The Medieval French Drama.* Oxford: Clarendon, 1954.

Frappier, J. *Chrétien de Troyes, The Man and His Work.* Trans. R. J. Cormier. Athens: Ohio Univ. Press, 1982.

———. *Etude sur la Mort le roi Artu.* 3d ed. Geneva: Droz, 1972.

Gaunt, S. *Troubadours and Irony.* Cambridge: Cambridge Univ. Press, 1989.

Gravdal, K. *Ravishing Maidens: Writing Rape in Medieval French Literature and Law.* Philadelphia: Univ. of Pennsylvania Press, 1991.

———. *Vilain and Courtois: Transgressive Parody in French Literature of the Twelfth and Thirteenth Centuries.* Lincoln: Univ. of Nebraska Press, 1989.

Green, D. *Irony in the Medieval Romance.* Cambridge: Cambridge Univ. Press, 1979.

Grimbert, J. *Yvain dans le miroir: Une poétique de la réflexion dans "Le Chevalier au lion" de Chrétien de Troyes.* Amsterdam: J. Benjamins, 1988.

Guiette, R. *Forme et senefiance.* Ed. J. Dufournet, M. de Grève, H. Braet. Geneva: Droz, 1978.

Haidu, P. *Aesthetic Distance in Chrétien de Troyes: Irony and Comedy in Cligès and Perceval.* Geneva: Droz, 1968.

———. *Lion-queue-coupée, l'écart symbolique chez Chrétien de Troyes.* Geneva: Droz, 1972.

Hanning, R. *The Individual in Twelfth-Century Romance.* New Haven: Yale Univ. Press, 1977.

Huchet, J-C. *Littérature médiévale et psychanalyse: Pour une clinique littéraire.* Paris: Presses Universitaires de France, 1990.

Huizinga, J. *The Waning of the Middle Ages: A Study of the Forms of Life, Thought and Art in France and the Netherlands in the XIVth and XVth Centuries.* Trans. F. Hopman. London: Arnold, 1924.

Hult, D. *Self-Fulfilling Prophecies: Readership and Authority in the First Roman de la Rose.* Cambridge: Cambridge Univ. Press, 1986.

Huot, S. *From Song to Book: The Poetics of Writing in Old French Lyric and Lyrical Narrative Poetry.* Ithaca: Cornell Univ. Press, 1987.

Jeanroy, A. *Les Origines de la poésie lyrique en France au Moyen Age.* Paris: Champion, 1889.

———. *La Poésie lyrique des troubadours.* 2 vols. Toulouse: Privat; Paris: Didier, 1934.

Johnson, L. *Poets as Players: Theme and Variation in Late Medieval French Poetry.* Stanford: Stanford Univ. Press, 1990.

Jung, M. R. *Etudes sur le poème allégorique en France au Moyen Age.* Berne: Francke, 1971.

Kay, S. *Subjectivity in Troubadour Poetry.* Cambridge: Cambridge Univ. Press, 1990.

Keller, H.-E., ed. *Romance Epic: Essays on a Medieval Literary Genre.* Kalamazoo, Mich.: The Medieval Institute, 1987.

Kelly, D. *The Art of Medieval French Romance.* Madison: Univ. of Wisconsin Press, 1992.

———. *Medieval Imagination: Rhetoric and the Poetry of Courtly Love.* Madison: Univ. of Wisconsin Press, 1978.

———, ed. *The Romances of Chrétien de Troyes: A Symposium.* Lexington, Ky.: French Forum, 1985.

Kendrick, L. *The Game of Love: Troubadour Word Play.* Berkeley: Univ. of California Press, 1988.

Kennedy, E. *Lancelot and the Grail: A Study of the Prose Lancelot.* Oxford: Clarendon, 1986.

Knight, A. *Aspects of Genre in Late Medieval French Drama.* Manchester: Manchester Univ. Press, 1983.

Köhler, E. *Ideal und Wirklichkeit in der höfischen Epik: Studien zur Form der frühen Artus- und Graldichtung.* 2d ed. Tübingen: Niemeyer, 1970. French trans., E. Kaufholz, *L'Aventure chevaleresque: Idéal et réalité dans le roman courtois.* Paris: Gallimard, 1974.

Lacy, N. J. *The Craft of Chrétien de Troyes: An Essay on Narrative Art.* Leiden: Brill, 1980.

Lacy, N. J., D. Kelly, and K. Busby, eds. *The Legacy of Chrétien de Troyes.* 2 vols. Amsterdam: Rodopi, 1987–88.

Lagorio, V., and M. L. Day, eds. *King Arthur Through the Ages.* New York: Garland, 1990.

Le Gentil, P. *La Chanson de Roland.* Paris: Hatier, 1962.

——. *Villon*. Paris: Hatier, 1967.

Le Goff, J. *The Medieval Imagination*. Trans. A. Goldhammer. Chicago: Univ. of Chicago Press, 1988.

Leupin, A. *Barbarolexis: Medieval Writing and Sexuality*. Cambridge, Mass.: Harvard Univ. Press, 1989.

Loomis, R. S. *Arthurian Tradition and Chrétien de Troyes*. New York: Columbia Univ. Press, 1949.

Lord, A. *The Singer of Tales*. Cambridge, Mass.: Harvard Univ. Press, 1960.

Lot, F. *Etude sur le Lancelot en prose*. Paris: Champion, 1918.

——. "Etudes sur les légendes épiques françaises IV: Le Cycle de Guillaume d'Orange." *Romania* 53 (1927): 449–73.

Luttrell, C. *The Creation of the First Arthurian Romance: A Quest*. Evanston: Northwestern Univ. Press, 1974.

Maddox, D. *The Arthurian Romances of Chrétien de Troyes: Once and Future Fictions*. Cambridge: Cambridge Univ. Press, 1991.

——. *Semiotics of Deceit: The Pathelin Era*. Lewisburg, Penn.: Bucknell Univ. Press, 1984.

——. *Structure and Sacring: The Systematic Kingdom in Chrétien's* Erec et Enide. Lexington, Ky.: French Forum, 1978.

Marx, J. *La Légende arthurienne et le Graal*. Paris: Presses Universitaires de France, 1952.

Méla, C. *Blanchefleur et le saint homme: Ou, la semblance des reliques*. Paris: Le Seuil, 1979.

——. *La Reine et le graal*. Paris: Le Seuil, 1981.

Menard, P. *Les Fabliaux, contes à rire du Moyen Age*. Paris: Presses Universitaires de France, 1983.

——. *Les Lais de Marie de France*. Paris: Presses Universitaires de France, 1979.

——. *Le Rire et le sourire dans le roman courtois en France au Moyen Age (1150–1250)*. Geneva: Droz, 1969.

Menéndez Pidál, R. *La Chanson de Roland y el neotradicionalismo (orígenes de la épica románica)*. Madrid: Espasa-Calpe, 1959. French trans., I.-M. Cluzel. *La Chanson de Roland et la tradition épique des Francs*. Paris: Picard, 1960.

Mickel, E. *Ganelon, Treason and the* Chanson de Roland. University Park, Penn.: Pennsylvania State Univ. Press, 1989.

Moelk, Univ. *Trobar clus, Trobar leu: Studien zur Dichtungstheorie der Trobadors*. Munich: W. Fink, 1968.

Muir, L. R. *Literature and Society in Medieval France: The Mirror and the Image, 1100–1500*. New York: St. Martin's, 1985.

Muscatine, C. *The Old French Fabliaux*. New Haven: Yale Univ. Press, 1986.

Nykrog, P. *L'Amour et la rose: Le grand dessein de Jean de Meun.* Lexington, Ky.: French Forum, 1986.

———. *Les Fabliaux: Etude d'histoire littéraire et de stylistique médiévale.* 2d ed. Geneva: Droz, 1973.

Paden, W. D., ed. *The Voice of the Trobairitz: Perspectives on the Women Troubadours.* Philadelphia: Univ. of Pennsylvania Press, 1989.

Page, C. *The Owl and the Nightingale: Musical Life and Ideas in France, 1100–1300.* Berkeley: Univ. of California Press, 1989.

———. *Voices and Instruments of the Middle Ages: Instrumental Practice and Songs in France, 1100–1300.* Berkeley: Univ. of California Press, 1986.

Paris, G. *Histoire poétique de Charlemagne.* Paris: Franck, 1865.

———. *La Littérature française au moyen âge: XIᵉ-XIVᵉ siècle.* Paris: Hachette, 1888.

Parry, M. *The Making of Homeric Verse.* Oxford: Clarendon, 1970.

Paterson, L. M. *Troubadours and Eloquence.* Oxford: Clarendon, 1975.

Patterson, L. *Negotiating the Past: The Historical Understanding of Medieval Literature.* Madison: Univ. of Wisconsin Press, 1987.

Payen, J.-Ch. *Le Motif du repentir dans la littérature française médiévale (des origines à 1230).* Geneva: Droz, 1967.

———. *Le Prince d'Aquitaine: Essai sur Guillaume IX, son oeuvre et son érotique.* Paris: Champion, 1980.

Poirion, D. *Le Merveilleux dans la littérature française du moyen âge.* Que sais-je? 1938. Paris: Presses Universitaires de France, 1982.

———. *Le Poète et le prince: L'évolution du lyrisme courtois de Guillaume de Machaut à Charles d'Orléans.* Paris: Presses Universitaires de France, 1965.

———. *Résurgences: Mythe et littérature à l'âge du symbole (XIIᵉ siècle).* Paris: Presses Universitaires de France, 1986.

———. *Le Roman de la Rose.* Paris: Hatier, 1973.

Poirion, D., and N. Regalado, eds. *Contexts: Style and Values in Medieval Art and Literature.* Yale French Studies, special issue. New Haven: Yale Univ. Press, 1991.

Rajna, P. *Le origini dell'epopea francese.* Florence: Sansoni, 1884.

Regalado, N. *Poetic Patterns in Rutebeuf: A Study in Non-Courtly Poetic Modes of the Thirteenth Century.* New Haven: Yale Univ. Press, 1970.

Rey-Flaud, H. *Le Cercle magique: Essai sur le théâtre en rond à la fin du moyen âge.* Paris: Gallimard, 1973.

———. *La Farce ou la machine à rire: Théorie d'un genre dramatique (1450–1550).* Geneva: Droz, 1984.

———. *La Névrose courtoise.* Paris: Navarin, 1983.

Rychner, J. *La Chanson de geste: Essai sur l'art épique des jongleurs.* Geneva: Droz, 1955.

Schenck, M. *The Fabliaux: Tales of Wit and Deception.* Amsterdam: Benjamins, 1987.

Schmolke-Hasselmann, B. *Der arthurische Versroman von Chrestien bis Froissart: Zur Geschichte einer Gattung.* Tübingen: M. Niemayer, 1980.

Shears, F. S. *Froissart, Chronicler and Poet.* London: G. Routledge & Sons, 1930.

Spence, S. *Rhetorics of Reason and Desire: Vergil, Augustine, and the Troubadours.* Ithaca: Cornell Univ. Press, 1988.

Spiegel, G. *The Chronicle Tradition of Saint-Denis: A Survey.* Brookline, Mass.: Classical Folia Editions, 1978.

———. *Romancing the Past: The Rise of Vernacular Prose Historiography in Thirteenth-Century France.* Berkeley: Univ. of California Press, 1993.

Stanesco, M. *Jeux d'errance du chevalier médiéval: Aspects ludiques de la foncion guerrière dans la littérature du Moyen Age flamboyant.* Leiden: Brill, 1988.

Strubel, A. *Le Roman de la Rose.* Paris: Presses Universitaires de France, 1984.

———. *La Rose, Renart et le Graal: La littérature allégorique en France au XIIIe siècle.* Paris: Champion, 1989.

Sturges, R. S. *Medieval Interpretation: Models of Reading in Literary Narrative, 1100–1500.* Carbondale: Southern Illinois Univ. Press, 1991.

Topsfield, L. *Troubadours and Love.* Cambridge: Cambridge Univ. Press, 1975.

Vance, E. *From Topic to Tale: Logic and Narrativity in the Middle Ages.* Minneapolis: Univ. of Minnesota Press, 1987.

———. *Mervelous Signals: Poetics and Sign Theory in the Middle Ages.* Lincoln: Univ. of Nebraska Press, 1986.

———. *Reading the Song of Roland.* Englewood Cliffs, N.J.: Prentice-Hall, 1970.

Van Vleck, A. *Memory and Re-creation in Troubadour Lyric.* Berkeley: Univ. of California Press, 1991.

Vinaver, E. *The Rise of Romance.* Oxford: Clarendon, 1971.

Vitz, E. *Medieval Narrative and Modern Narratology: Subjects and Objects of Desire.* New York: New York Univ. Press, 1989.

Zink, M. *La Subjectivité littéraire: Autour du siècle de saint Louis.* Paris: Presses Universitaires de France, 1985.

Zumthor, P. *Langue, text, énigme.* Paris: Le Seuil, 1975.

———. *La Lettre et la voix: De la "littérature" médiévale.* Paris: Le Seuil, 1987.

———. *Le Masque et la lumière: La poétique des grands rhétoriqueurs.* Paris: Le Seuil, 1978.

———. *Oral Poetry: An Introduction*. Trans. K. Murphy-Judy. Minneapolis: Univ. of Minnesota Press, 1990.

———. *Speaking of the Middle Ages*. Trans. S. White. Lincoln: Univ. of Nebraska Press, 1986.

———. *Toward a Medieval Poetics*. Trans. P. Bennett. Minneapolis: Univ. of Minnesota Press, 1992.

———. "Un trompe-l'oeil linguistique? Le Refrain de *L'aube bilingue de Fleury*." *Romania* 105 (1984): 171–92.

Chronology

Not every work mentioned in the text is included in this Chronology, only the most important or those that were the first of their genre. The dates of some important events in western European history and of some well-known literary works from the other western European national traditions have been included for the sake of comparison and reference.

c. 675	Caedmon's Hymn
731	Bede, *Historia Ecclesiastica gentis Anglorum* (*Ecclesiastical History of the English People*)
c. 750	*Beowulf*
c. 800	*Hildebrandslied* (*The Song of Hildebrand*)
814	DEATH OF CHARLEMAGNE
c. 830	*Heliand* and *Muspilli*
842	Oaths of Strasbourg
843	TREATY OF VERDUN DIVIDES CAROLINGIAN EMPIRE
871–899	REIGN OF ALFRED THE GREAT (England)
c. 881–882	*Séquence de sainte Eulalie* (*Sequence of Saint Eulalie*)
910	CLUNY ABBEY FOUNDED
936–973	REIGN OF OTTO I THE GREAT (Germany)
c. 950	Sermon on the Book of Jonah
c. 960–980	Hrotswitha von Gandersheim writes plays
962	OTTO I CROWNED HOLY ROMAN EMPEROR
982	ERIC THE RED COLONIZES GREENLAND
987	CORONATION OF HUGUES CAPET
c. 950–1000	*Passion* of Clermont
	Vie de saint Léger (*Life of Saint Leger*)
c. 1000	LEIF ERICSSON LANDS IN NOVA SCOTIA
1000–1035	REIGN OF SANCHO III THE GREAT (Spain)
c. 1050	*Chanson de sainte Foy d'Agen* (*Song of Saint Foy of Agen*)
	Vie de saint Alexis (*Life of Saint Alexis*)
	Ruodlieb
1054	SEPARATION OF THE EASTERN (ORTHODOX) AND WESTERN (ROMAN) CHURCHES

1066	BATTLE OF HASTINGS
1075	POPE GREGORY VII PROHIBITS THE LAY IN VESTITURE OF BISHOPS
1085–1086	DOMESDAY BOOK COMPILED
1095–1099	FIRST CRUSADE
c. 1100	The first *chansons de geste*: *Roland, Gormont et Isembart, Guillaume d'Orange.*
	The first troubadour: William IX (1071–1127)
1115–1153	SAINT BERNARD ABBOT OF CLAIRVAUX
c. 1120–1140	Troubadours: Marcabru, Cercamon, Jaufré Rudel
1122	CONCORDAT OF WORMS (end of Investiture Controversy)
1122–1152	SUGER ABBOT OF SAINT-DENIS
1127	MURDER OF CHARLES THE GOOD, COUNT OF FLANDERS
1130–1154	REIGN OF ROGER II OF SICILY
c. 1140	*Cantar de mío Cid* (*Poem of the Cid*)
c. 1135	Albéric de Pisançon, *Roman d'Alexandre* (*Romance of Alexander*)
1136	Geoffrey of Monmouth, *Historia regum Britanniae* (*History of the Kings of Britain*)
1141	Ordericus Vitalis, *Historia ecclesiastica* (*Ecclesiastical History*)
1147–1150	SECOND CRUSADE
c. 1140–1170	Troubadours: Bernard de Ventadour, Pierre d'Auvergne, Raimbaud d'Orange
1148	Bernard Silvester, *Cosmographia* (*On Cosmogony*)
c. 1150	*Jeu d'Adam* (*Play of Adam*)
1152	LOUIS VIII REPUDIATES ELEANOR OF AQUITAINE, WHO THEN MARRIES HENRY II PLANTAGENET
1152–1190	REIGN OF FREDERICK I BARBAROSSA (Holy Roman Empire)
1154–1189	REIGN OF HENRY II (England)
1155	Wace, *Roman de Brut* (*Romance of Brut*)
c. 1155–1170	*Roman de Thèbes* (*Romance of Thebes*)
	Roman d'Enéas (*Romance of Aeneas*)
	Benoît de Sainte-Maure, *Roman de Troie* (*Romance of Troy*)
1160	Alan of Lille, *De planctu Naturae* (*The Complaint of Nature*)
1170	MURDER OF THOMAS BECKET
c. 1170	Marie de France, *Lais* (*Lays*)
	Chrétien de Troyes, *Erec et Enide* (*Erec and Enide*)
c. 1170–1175	Thomas, *Tristan*

	First branches of the *Roman du Renart* (*Romance of Renart*)
	Gautier d'Arras, *Ille et Galeron* (*Ille and Galeron*), *Eracle*
	Eilhart von Oberg, *Tristan*
c. 1175–1186	Heinrich von Veldeke, *Aeneid*
c. 1176–1181	Chrétien de Troyes, *Cligès*, *Le Chevalier de la charrette* (*The Knight of the Cart*), *Le Chevalier au lion* (*The Knight with the Lion*)
1179–1223	REIGN OF PHILIPPE-AUGUSTE
1180	Alain of Lille, *Anticlaudianus*
	Herzog Ernst (*Count Ernst*)
c. 1180–1200	Trouvères: Châtelain de Coucy, Gace Brulé, Conon de Béthune
	Minnesingers: Heinrich von Morungen, Reinmar von Hagenau, Walther von der Vogelweide
	Béroul, *Tristan*
	Hélinand de Froidmont, *Vers de la Mort* (*Verses on Death*)
	Hartmann von Aue, *Erec*
c. 1185	Chrétien de Troyes, *Le Conte du Graal* (*The Story of the Grail*)
1187	SALADIN RETAKES JERUSALEM
1191	THIRD CRUSADE
c. 1195	Hartmann von Aue, *Der Arme Heinrich* (*Poor Heinrich*)
c. 1200	Jean Bodel, *Jeu de saint Nicolas* (*Play of Saint Nicholas*)
	Robert de Boron, *Estoire dou Graal* (*Story of the Grail*)
	Jean Renart, *L'Escoufle* (*The Kite*), *Lai de l'Ombre* (*Lay of the Shadow*)
	Nibelungenlied (*Song of the Nibelungs*)
	The Owl and the Nightingale
1202	FOURTH CRUSADE
	Jean Bodel, *Congés* (*Farewells*)
	Hartmann von Aue, *Iwein*
1204	CONSTANTINOPLE TAKEN BY THE CRUSADERS
c. 1205	Wirnt von Grafenberg, *Wigalois*
	Layamon, *Brut*
1209	BEGINNING OF THE ALBIGENSIAN CRUSADE
c. 1210	Chronicles of Robert de Clari and Villehardouin
	Wolfram von Eschenbach, *Parzival*
	Gottfried von Strassburg, *Tristan*
	Gudrun
1212	BATTLE OF NAVAS DE TOLOSA, ALMOHADS DEFEATED BY ALFONSO VIII OF CASTILE

1212–1213	Guillaume de Tudèle, *Chanson de la croisade albigeoise* (*Song of the Albigensian Crusade*) (first part)
1214	BATTLE OF BOUVINES
1215	FOURTH LATERAN COUNCIL
	MAGNA CARTA
c. 1215	Heinrich von dem Türlin, *Diu Krone* (*The Crown*)
	Der Stricker, *Daniel von blühenden Tal* (*Daniel from the Blooming Valley*)
1219	*Chanson de la croisade albigeoise* (*Song of the Albigensian Crusade*) (second part)
c. 1220–1230	Gautier de Coincy, *Miracles de Notre Dame* (*Miracles of Our Lady*)
	Prose *Lancelot*
	Perlesvaus
	Jean Renart, *Guillaume de Dole*
	Guillaume de Lorris, *Le Roman de la Rose* (*The Romance of the Rose*)
1226–1270	REIGN OF SAINT LOUIS
c. 1230	*Queste del saint Graal* (*Quest for the Holy Grail*)
	Mort le roi Artu (*Death of King Arthur*)
	Prose *Tristan* (first version)
1248	SEVENTH CRUSADE
1250	CAPTIVITY OF SAINT LOUIS
	Wernher the Gardener, *Meier Helmbrecht*
1252–1284	ALFONSO X THE WISE, KING OF CASTILE
1254–1259	Quarrel of the University of Paris
	Rutebeuf's poems on the University
before 1267	Brunetto Latini, *Livre du trésor* (*Book of Treasure*)
1272–1307	REIGN OF EDWARD I (England)
1276–1277	Adam de la Halle, *Jeu de la feuillée* (*Play of the Bower*)
1282	SICILIAN VESPERS (French expelled from Sicily)
1291	FALL OF SAINT-JEAN D'ACRE
1298	Marco Polo, *Livre des merveilles* (*Book of Wonders*)
c. 1300	*Libro del Caballero Zifar* (*Book of Sir Zifar*)
1302	MATINS OF BRUGES
	BATTLE OF THE GOLDEN SPURS
c. 1306	Dante begins work on the *Divina commedia*
1309	THE POPE MOVES TO AVIGNON
	Joinville, *Vie de saint Louis* (*Life of Saint Louis*)
1324–1328	PEASANTS' REVOLT IN FLANDERS
1327–1377	REIGN OF EDWARD III (England)
1328	PHILIPPE VI OF VALOIS BECOMES KING; END OF CAPETIAN LINE
	Guilhem Molinier, *Leys d'Amors* (*Lay of Love*)

1330	Juan Ruiz (Archpriest of Hita), *Libro de buen amor* (*Book of Good Love*)
1335	Prince Juan Manuel of Castile, *Libro de los exemplos del Conde Lucanor* (*Count Lucanor*)
1337	HUNDRED YEARS' WAR BEGINS
1338–1345	JACQUES VAN ARTEVELDE RULES GHENT
1340	BATTLE OF L'ECLUSE
	Machaut, *Le Remède de Fortune* (*The Remedy for Fortune*)
c. 1340	*Perceforest*
1341	PETRARCH CROWNED POET LAUREATE IN ROME
1346	BATTLE OF CRÉCY
	Machaut, *Le Jugement du roi de Bohême* (*The Judgement of the King of Bohemia*)
1348–1350	BLACK DEATH, FLAGELLANTS, PERSECUTIONS
	ORDER OF THE GARTER FOUNDED
	Machaut, *Le Jugement du roi de Navarre* (*The Judgement of the King of Navarre*)
1351–53	Boccaccio, *Decameron*
1356	BATTLE OF POITIERS, CAPTIVITY OF JEAN II
	CHARLES IV ISSUES GOLDEN BULL (setting forth method for electing emperor)
1356–1358	PARIS UPRISING LED BY ETIENNE MARCEL
	JACQUERIE
	Pierre Bersuire's translation of Livy
	Machaut, *Le Confort d'Ami* (*The Friend's Comfort*)
1360	TREATY OF BRÉTIGNY
	Machaut, *La Prison amoureuse* (*The Amorous Prison*)
	Alliterative *Morte Arthure*
1362	PHILIP III THE BOLD BECOMES DUKE OF BURGUNDY
	Machaut, *Le Voir dit* (*The True* Dit)
1364	REIGN OF CHARLES V BEGINS
c. 1369	Froissart, *L'Espinette amoureuse* (*The Amorous Hawthorn*)
	Chaucer, *Book of the Duchess*
1370	DU GUESCLIN NAMED CONNÉTABLE
1370–1387	William Langland, *Piers Plowman*
1373	Froissart, first book of the *Chroniques* (*Chronicles*)
c. 1375	*Sir Gawain and the Green Knight, Pearl, Patience, Purity*
1376	*Le Songe du Verger* (*The Dream of the Orchard*)
1378	GREAT SCHISM BEGINS
1380	REIGN OF CHARLES VI BEGINS
	DEATH OF DU GUESCLIN

	Froissart, *Méliador*
	Cuvelier, *Vie de Bertrand du Guesclin (Life of Bertrand du Guesclin)*
	The Cloud of Unknowing
1381	PEASANTS' REVOLT IN ENGLAND
c. 1385	Chaucer, *Troilus and Criseyde*
c. 1387	Chaucer begins work on *The Canterbury Tales*
1389	Philippe de Mézières, *Songe du vieil pélerin (Dream of the Old Pilgrim)*
	Honoré Bonet, *L'Arbre des batailles (The Tree of Battles)*
c. 1390	John Gower, *Confessio Amantis*
	Julian of Norwich, *Revelations of Divine Love*
1392	CHARLES VI'S MADNESS BEGINS
	Eustache Deschamps, *Art de dictier et de faire chansons (Art of Versifying and Making Songs)*
1394	BIRTH OF CHARLES D'ORLÉANS
1396	GERSON BECOMES CHANCELLOR OF THE UNIVERSITY OF PARIS
	SIEGE AND DEFEAT OF NICOPOLIS
c. 1400	*Les Quinze Joies du Mariage (The Fifteen Joys of Marriage)*
	Monstrelet, *Chroniques* (1400–1444)
	Johannes von Tepl, *Der Ackermann aus Böhmen (The Bohemian Plowman)*
	QUARREL OF THE *ROMAN DE LA ROSE*
1404	DEATH OF PHILIP THE BOLD
	Christine de Pizan, *Livre de mutacion de Fortune (Book of Fortune's Change)*
1405	*Journal d'un bourgeois de Paris (Journal of a Parisian Burgher)* (1405–1449)
1407	ASSASSINATION OF LOUIS D'ORLÉANS
1408	Christine de Pizan, *Livre du corps de policie (Book of the Body of Policy)*
	Livre des faits du maréchal de Boucicaut (Book of the Deeds of the Marshal de Boucicaut)
1415	BATTLE OF AGINCOURT, CAPTIVITY OF CHARLES D'ORLÉANS
1419	ASSASSINATION OF JEAN THE FEARLESS, DUKE OF BURGUNDY
	Georges Chastellain, *Chroniques* (1419–1475)
1420	TREATY OF TROYES
1422	DEATH OF CHARLES VI
	Alain Chartier, *Le Quadrilogue invectif (The Vituperative Quadrilogue)*

	Bucarius, *Le Pastoralet*
1424	Alain Chartier, *La Belle Dame sans mercy* (*The Beautiful Lady without Pity*)
c. 1425	Margery Kempe, *The Book of Margery Kempe*
1429	CORONATION OF CHARLES VII
	Christine de Pizan, *Ditié de Jeanne d'Arc* (*Poem of Joan of Arc*)
1430	CREATION OF THE ORDER OF THE GOLDEN FLEECE
1431	EXECUTION OF JOAN OF ARC
1435	TREATY OF ARRAS
	Olivier de la Marche, *Mémoires* (1435–88)
1437	Charles d'Orléans, *La Departie d'Amour* (*Farewell to Love*)
1440	CHARLES D'ORLÉANS FREED
1444	Juan de Mena, *El laberinto de Fortuna* (*The Labyrinth of Fortune*)
1450	JACK CADE'S REBELLION (England)
1452	Arnoul Gréban, *Mystère de la Passion* (*Mystery of the Passion*)
1453	CONSTANTINOPLE CAPTURED BY THE TURKS
1454	BANQUET OF THE PHEASANT
	PEACE OF LODI BETWEEN VENICE AND MILAN
1455–1485	WARS OF THE ROSES
1456	REINSTATEMENT OF JOAN OF ARC
	Villon, *Lais* (*Bequests*)
	Antoine de La Sale, *Jehan de Saintré*
1457	René d'Anjou, *Livre du cuer d'Amour espris* (*The Book of the Heart Inflamed with Love*)
1458	David Aubert, *Chroniques et conquestes de Charlemagne* (*Chronicles and Conquests of Charlemagne*)
1461	REIGN OF LOUIS XI BEGINS
	Villon, *Testament*
1465	DEATH OF CHARLES D'ORLÉANS
	Farce de maître Pathelin (*Farce of Master Pathelin*)
c. 1465	*Les Cent nouvelles nouvelles* (*The One Hundred New Novellas*)
1469–1492	LORENZO DE' MEDICI RULES FLORENCE
1470	FIRST PRINTING PRESS INSTALLED IN THE SORBONNE
	Mystère des actes des Apôtres (*Mystery of the Acts of the Apostles*)
c. 1470	Sir Thomas Malory, *Le Morte Darthur*
1474	REIGN OF ISABELLA I OF CASTILE BEGINS
c. 1475	*Everyman*

Index